Comments on other *Amazing Stories* from readers & reviewers

"Tightly written volumes filled with lots of wit and humour about famous and infamous Canadians."
Eric Shackleton, *The Globe and Mail*

"The heightened sense of drama and intrigue, combined with a good dose of human interest is what sets Amazing Stories *apart."*
Pamela Klaffke, *Calgary Herald*

"This is popular history as it should be... For this price, buy two and give one to a friend."
Terry Cook, a reader from Ottawa, on **Rebel Women**

"Glasner creates the moment of the explosion itself in graphic detail...she builds detail upon gruesome detail to create a convincingly authentic picture."
Peggy McKinnon, *The Sunday Herald*, on **The Halifax Explosion**

"It was wonderful...I found I could not put it down. I was sorry when it was completed."
Dorothy F. from Manitoba on **Marie-Anne Lagimodière**

"Stories are rich in description, and bristle with a clever, stylish realness."
Mark Weber, *Central Alberta Advisor*, on **Ghost Town Stories II**

"A compelling read. Bertin...has selected only the most intriguing tales, which she narrates with a wealth of detail."
Joyce Glasner, *New Brunswick Reader*, on **Strange Events**

"The resulting book is one readers will want to share with all the women in their lives."
Lynn Martel, *Rocky Mountain Outlook*, on **Women Explorers**

ALEXANDER GRAHAM BELL

ALEXANDER GRAHAM BELL

The Spirit of Invention

BIOGRAPHY

by Jennifer Groundwater

PUBLISHED BY ALTITUDE PUBLISHING CANADA LTD.
1500 Railway Avenue, Canmore, Alberta T1W 1P6
www.altitudepublishing.com
1-800-957-6888

Publisher	Stephen Hutchings
Associate Publisher	Kara Turner
Series Editor	Jill Foran
Editor	Deborah Lawson
Digital Photo Colouring	Bryan Pezzi

We acknowledge the financial support of the Government
of Canada through the Book Publishing Industry Development
Program (BPIDP) for our publishing activities.

Altitude GreenTree Program
Altitude Publishing will plant twice as many trees as were used
in the manufacturing of this product.

We acknowledge the support of the Canada Council for the Arts which
in 2003 invested $21.7 million in writing and publishing throughout Canada.

Canada Council   Conseil des Arts
for the Arts   du Canada

National Library of Canada Cataloguing in Publication Data

Groundwater, Jennifer
Alexander Graham Bell / Jennifer Groundwater.

(Amazing stories)
ISBN 1-55439-006-0

1. Bell, Alexander Graham, 1847-1922. 2.
Inventors--Canada--Biography.
3. Inventors--United States--Biography. I. Title. II. Series: Amazing
stories (Canmore, Alta.)

TK6143.B4G76 2005   621.385'092   C2004-906272-7

An application for the trademark for Amazing Stories™
has been made and the registered trademark is pending.

Printed and bound in Canada by Friesens
2 4 6 8 9 7 5 3

This book is dedicated to my parents,
Jim and Marion Groundwater, for always
lovingly believing in each other and in me.

Contents

Alexander Graham Bell, ca. 1914–1919

Prologue

It was 8:15 p.m., a quarter of an hour after the time they had agreed on. The large crowd of curious townspeople buzzed with chatter, oblivious to the consternation of the intense young man in their midst. He was hoping to hear his Uncle David's voice coming over the wire as arranged, but something wasn't right.

Alec had carefully planned a musical programme for the evening to demonstrate his new invention to the citizens of Paris, Ontario. The transmitter was set up at the Brantford telegraph office, some 13 kilometres away. There, Alec's uncle and several other willing participants were going to entertain the listeners in Paris.

At the moment, they were singing their hearts out in Brantford, not knowing that at the other end of the line, all that could be heard were "explosive sounds like the discharge of distant artillery" coming through the receiver. The din was deafening.

Alec's heart sank. What could be wrong? He had already done two other long-distance tests of his apparatus with what he considered "perfect success." Now, in front of all the local notables, he was going to look a perfect fool.

Suddenly he had a brain wave. The problem must be

the electromagnetic coils. He turned to the telegraph operator standing by and asked him to telegraph a message to
Brantford: "Quickly, change the magnet on your transmitter
to a higher resistance." He did the same to his receiver. He was
almost afraid of what he might hear, but, to his great relief, this
time "the vocal sounds came out clearly and strongly."

Dramatically, he invited the members of the audience to
listen to entertainers a full 13 kilometres away, something that
had never before happened in the history of the world ...

Chapter 1
"A Great and Glorious Success"

t was June 1876 in Philadelphia. In a quiet corner of a massive hall, a small device went almost unnoticed by the crowds thronging through the displays of the Centennial Exhibition. The inventor of the device, a young Scottish teacher of the deaf, was away from his display, busy exploring the wonders of the fair. He was in Philadelphia for only a few days. Tomorrow his exhibit would go before the judges of the electrical displays, and then he had to be on a train home to Boston immediately afterwards.

The inventor's name was Alexander Graham Bell, and his life was about to change radically.

That year in Philadelphia, Americans were celebrating. It was the 100th anniversary of the signing of the Declaration of Independence, and the nation had decided to throw a huge party — the first world's fair to be held on American soil. It was called the Centennial Exhibition, and it was a world's fair without compare, a showcase of all the good things progress had brought to America. It ran from May to November, attracting an amazing nine million visitors. (The population of the country was only 46 million at the time.)

Thirty-seven countries came to participate. Several erected permanent buildings on the 285 acres of land along the Schuylkill River, while others put up buildings within the Main Exhibition Hall. There were over 250 buildings in all.

The world's fair opened on May 10, 1876, in front of a crowd of 150,000 people. After a selection of stirring patriotic music and a 1000-gun artillery salute, President Ulysses S. Grant, accompanied by the Brazilian emperor, Dom Pedro, and his wife, Empress Teresa, officially declared the Exhibition open.

At a length of 1876 feet, or over half a kilometre, the great glass and steel Main Exhibition Hall was the largest building in the world at the time. Within the main hall were a staggering number of exhibits. It would take at least two to three days to see all the wonders exhibited at the fair, from the world's first monorail to a massive Corliss steam engine that powered any number of machines on display within Machinery Hall.

The fair was notable for the sheer number of things on display. Visitors could marvel at recent inventions such as

"A Great and Glorious Success"

the typewriter and the electric light bulb. There were oddities such as a solid silver table from Brazil, the arm and torch of the Statue of Liberty (at this point the whole statue was not completed), and a log cabin from Canada. And, tucked away in the Education section of the Main Hall, was Alexander Graham Bell's telephone.

Alec had arrived at the fair under great protest. He hadn't wanted to demonstrate the telephone in the first place, believing it was not really ready to be presented to the world. He didn't mind showing it to other scientists, who would probably accept a few hiccups since they understood the nature of invention. But he felt the public at large would expect perfection, and he was far from sure that the telephone would stand up to such exacting scrutiny.

His fiancée, Mabel Hubbard, and her father, Gardiner Greene Hubbard — who both had an aptitude for business and marketing far beyond his own — realized how critical it was for Alec to be at the fair. It was the ideal venue to launch such an exciting new product. The stubborn Scotsman had maintained that he himself would not attend, but he had finally agreed to enter the telephone as an exhibit. However, by the time he made up his mind, the deadline for entering a technological display had passed — which is how the telephone ended up in the Education section, along with the display of Alec's other passions, teaching the deaf and Visible Speech.

Mabel had begun persuading her fiancé with gentle

inducements. She reminded the reluctant Alec that the judging of the scientific exhibits was coming up in a few days' time, and that among the judges was William Thomson (later Lord Kelvin), one of the world's most famous physicists. His theoretical and practical work in laying the first transatlantic submarine cable had already earned him a knighthood. He was a most influential person. It wouldn't do to have Thomson examine the apparatus without the inventor being there.

Alec was overworked, as usual. In addition to being a part-time inventor, he had plenty of other commitments in Boston. He was a teacher to several deaf students, and he also had a school where he taught would-be teachers of the deaf. In addition, he was a professor at Boston University's School of Oratory, where he taught vocal physiology and elocution. Like most academics, he was always very busy in June with coursework and exams. He resented having to take time out from what he considered to be his true work to be at the fair. He arranged for Mabel's cousin Willie, who had been helping him in his lab, to go in his place.

But all his protests were useless in the face of Mabel's final wily persuasion. One warm June evening, she took him down to the train station, supposedly to wish Willie well as he set off on his trip to Philadelphia. Unbeknownst to her fiancé, she had packed his bag and arranged for a ticket for him, as well as accommodation in Philadelphia. On the way there, she kept encouraging him to go instead of Willie, but Alec was insistent. He had to be in Boston to give his teaching students their year-end exam. Still debating the point, they made it as far as the platform from which the train was about to depart. Suddenly, Mabel burst into a flood of tears. She told Alec that she would break off their engagement if he didn't love her enough to do this one thing for her.

What could he do? He got on the train.

Once in Philadelphia, Alec checked into the Grande Villa Hotel, anxiously thinking about his exams and students at home rather than the Centennial Exhibition. His telephone had been rather damaged along the way. One piece had disappeared altogether. He hunted high and low for it, finally finding it damaged, but repairable. He had his work cut out for him to get it in working order before the judging.

However, he did find some time to speak with the judges and tell them about his work. He had a grand discussion with one of them in his hotel the night he arrived. He also introduced himself to William Thomson, right in the middle of Thomson's examination of Elisha Gray's machine. He was delighted to hear Thomson's "good broad Scotch accent," and joked in a letter to Mabel that ties of shared nationality might give him an edge in the judging. (Elisha Gray, who was one of Alec's chief inventing competitors in telegraphy, was American. A former carpenter, Gray had patented several improvements to the telegraph and by the summer of 1874 had invented a "musical telegraph" that would transmit melodies long-distance over wires. This was the machine Gray had on display at the fair.)

Thomson told Alec to be at the Exhibition on Sunday, June 25, when he would be coming to the fair with Dom Pedro and the other judges to see Gray's work; he wished to examine Alec's work that day as well.

Alec was nervous, feeling unprepared to do battle with his rival. "I don't like this at all," he thought. "I would rather avoid a direct collision with Mr. Gray if possible." However, he was confident he could hold his own when discussing theory, even if his machine were to fail him at a crucial moment.

After he set up his display he wrote to Mabel, telling her of the wonders of the Centennial. "It is so prodigious and so wonderful that it absolutely staggers one," he mused. "Just think of having the products of all the nations condensed into a few acres of buildings." He wished she were there to see it with him, though he kidded that he was glad she couldn't see the jewellery display, fearing she "would never be satisfied with any ordinary income after that."

On Sunday, Alec was as ready as he could be. He had already strung up telegraph wire in the Exhibition Hall, and had arranged to "borrow" power from the Atlantic and Pacific Telegraph Company. But he was still apprehensive about going head to head with Gray, whose "musical telegraph" was prominently featured as part of the Western Electric Company's big-bucks display.

The day was hot and muggy. One disadvantage of the massive glass Exhibition Hall was that, on fine days, the sun beat down on the building and heated it up beyond comfort. Alec, who hated warm weather anyway, was feeling sick from heat and nerves as he watched Sir William Thomson and his entourage of about 50 people take in Elisha Gray's demonstration.

Once Gray's presentation got underway, Alec felt somewhat reassured. Gray was not a man of science and had to get a professor to explain how his apparatus worked. Showing his frugal roots, Alec dismissed Gray's method for transmitting musical notes as too expensive. "It must have cost from $15.00 to $20.00 per note to produce ... I accomplished the same thing by means of instruments costing two cents per note." Gray also attempted to send two messages at once, but Alec was not impressed with his attempt. The audience, however, was transfixed by the musical demonstration, so the whole thing took a great deal of time.

While Gray was doing his demonstration, Alec caught the emperor's eye and gave him a wave. Dom Pedro had visited Alec's school for teachers in Boston a few weeks previously, and had seemed very interested in the education of deaf children. Now, he recognized Alec and brought the entourage over to his exhibit once Gray had finished his demonstration.

The judges were hot and weary after a full day of looking at exhibits. They nearly decided to pack it in after Gray's lengthy demonstration. If they had, it would have been impossible for Alec to be there in person when they visited his display, for he absolutely had to be on the train home that evening.

Fortunately, Dom Pedro saved the day by coming over to Alec and greeting him warmly. "How do you do, Professor Bell? What are you doing here? How are the deaf mutes of Boston?" When Alec explained what he had to show, Dom Pedro went back to the group and asked them to look at just one more exhibit, since he knew the inventor.

First, Alec showed his multiple telegraph and succeeded in transmitting two messages at once. He then explained his theory of the telephone and undulating current, and offered to demonstrate. "This is an invention 'in embryo,'" he hedged, in case no vocal sounds were heard. He then went off to his transmitter, which he had set up some distance away. Willie Hubbard waited at the receiver in front of the judges and other hangers-on.

Sir William listened at the receiver, and repeated Alec's words with astonishment: "Do you understand what I say," he muttered. He looked up wildly and said, "Where is Mr. Bell? I must see Mr. Bell!" and ran off towards Alec, in the direction indicated by Willie. When he found Alec at the transmitter he told him to recite something, and then returned to the receiver. Alec began, "To be or not to be, that is the question ..." Thomson listened a while longer, then passed the receiver to the emperor, who was equally overcome, saying, "I have heard, I have heard."

"It was a great and glorious success," exulted Alec in a

letter to his parents a few days later. Willie did a follow-up display for the judges after Alec had returned to Boston. The machine was so astounding that the scientists had to be sure there was no trickery involved, that it was genuine. But it worked just as well the next time, even though the transmitter had been moved and set up in a new location as a safeguard against a hoax. Thomson and another judge tested it thoroughly to prevent any controversy.

Alec was rewarded with the Centennial medal for his invention, which Thomson declared to be "the most wonderful thing I have seen in America." The young teacher returned to Boston in a happy daze. He and Elisha Gray had talked and agreed to join forces, which Alec rightly felt meant "fame and fortune to both of us." The telephone had passed its first major test with flying colours. Now Alec had exam papers to grade.

Chapter 2
"Why Don't You Do Something Useful?"

hile the telephone was Alec's first invention to gain recognition, it was by no means the first thing he had ever created from scratch. In a way, his whole life so far had led up to the dramatic moment at the Centennial where he recited "To be or not to be."

As a youth, Alec already possessed a quick mind and good problem-solving skills. He and his friend Ben Herdman were fond of goofing around at the flour mill managed by Ben's father. One day, Mr. Herdman took the boys into his office and gave them a "good talking-to. He wound up with the words, 'Now, boys, why don't you do something useful?'"

When Alec asked what he could do, Mr. Herdman mused, "If only you could take the husks off this wheat you would be of some help."

In the days that followed, Alec rose to this rather strange challenge. He scrubbed the damp grains with a stiff nailbrush until the husks were gone. He then suggested to Mr. Herdman that a wire-lined vat already installed in the mill would do a similar job for large quantities of grain — and he was right! This was his very first invention.

Not long after this, young Alexander Bell took the unusual step of augmenting his birth name. When a Canadian visitor named Alexander Graham boarded with them for a time, Alec decided the boarder's name had a fine ring to it. And so, on his 11th birthday, the family drank a toast to the newly self-christened Alexander *Graham* Bell. From then on he was still Alec to the family, but often went by A. Graham Bell or Graham Bell later on in life. (This wasn't the only adjustment he made to his name. As a lad, Alexander had spelled the short form of his name with a "k" on the end — "Aleck." But much later, when he began courting his sweetie, Mabel, she asked him to drop the "k" at the end of his nickname — and he granted her request.)

* * *

Several years later, a teenage Alec stood gazing in disbelief at his reflection in the looking glass. Used to wearing comfortable Scottish tweeds to roam through the countryside near Edinburgh, he suddenly found himself kitted out as a young

London dandy, complete with a tall silk hat, kid gloves, and — worst of all — a cane. Alexander Bell, Alec's grandfather, believed one should always leave the house dressed as a gentleman, even if it was only for an hour's walk in the private gardens across the road. As soon as Alec had arrived in his tweedy Scottish best, Alexander Bell had called for a tailor and had bought his grandson the items necessary to a gentleman.

It was 1862, and 15-year-old Alexander Graham Bell had come to live in London with his grandfather for a year.

Through his life so far, the young Scotsman had demonstrated both uncommon intelligence and uncommonly poor scholastic performance. He was very interested in botany and "natural history" as pastimes, but he found his classes dull, which made him a mediocre student. His parents felt that a year with his grandfather would help him shape up and would keep the older Alexander from feeling too lonely after the death of his second wife. It was to be a turning point in young Alec's life.

His grandfather lived a comfortable life in a posh part of London, and he earned his living teaching elocution — helping cure stammers and improve people's spoken English. Considering he had begun life as a shoemaker in rural Scotland, Alexander Bell had done very well for himself indeed.

Alexander Bell Senior fired up his grandson intellectually, getting him interested in reading more deeply than the lad had ever done before. Alec's elocution was greatly improved by the memorization and recitation of many passages from the works of William Shakespeare. He went to dinner parties where he mingled with the leading intellectuals of the day. Once he even dined with European royalty. By the time he returned home to Edinburgh a year later, he looked and acted much older than his age.

Before Alec left London, he and his father met with Sir Charles Wheatstone, who was renowned for his work in sound, telegraphy, and music. Wheatstone demonstrated to the Bells his speaking machine, which he had created using an earlier design by another scientist. The automaton made a great impression on Alec, who "heard it pronounce, in a very mechanical manner, several simple words and sentences." Wheatstone then gave Alec the designs he had used. In typical Alec fashion he looked at them and thought, "I can do better than this."

Alec's father, Melville, offered to pay for the supplies needed and offered a "big prize" to Alec and his older brother, Melly, if they managed to build one of these automatons for themselves. The boys decided to have a go. Alec took responsibility for building the tongue and mouth, complete with a soft palate and teeth, while Melly made the lungs, throat, and larynx.

This project brought the boys closer together as they fiddled with materials and researched how best to make the thing speak. They based the insides of the model as closely as possible on the human head — Alec somehow obtained a real skull to use as a model — though they didn't spend much time on giving it facial features. By manipulating the "lips," positioning the "tongue," and blowing into the machine, they were able to get it to sound "like a baby in great distress," crying "Mamma" over and over in the shared hallway of their home, until one of their tenants was heard to inquire, "Good gracious, what can be the matter with that baby?" The boys then slipped away with the machine to giggle triumphantly over the results of their practical joke.

At 18 and 16 years old, Melly and Alec were having a tough time at home. Melville Bell was very authoritarian, and his intense devotion to his chosen profession was somewhat formidable. Like most teenage boys, the brothers experienced friction with their father and found it hard to live up to his demands. In Alec's case, after a year in London of relative freedom (aside from Grandfather Bell's dress code), going back to being an unquestioningly obedient son was almost impossible. He loved and revered his father, but they didn't always understand each other.

Alec resolved to run away to sea. He packed a bag and made plans to head for the docks to select a suitable ship on which to stow away, but "better thought prevailed" and he decided to look for a regular job instead. Perusing the newspapers, he found that a school in Elgin, in the northeast of Scotland, was seeking two teachers, one of elocution and one of music. He decided to apply for the music position while Melly applied for the elocution position. They gave their father's name as a reference, since neither of them had had a real job before.

After several long discussions with their father, Melly decided to go to university instead, and Alec became a teacher. He set off for the Weston House Academy to teach both elocution and music. At only 16 years of age, Alec was younger than many of his students. But due to his serious demeanour, distinctive speaking voice, and the London polish instilled by his grandfather, his pupils never guessed his true age. He turned out to be an able teacher and his students did well under his guidance. Perhaps his memories of dull teachers only a few years earlier had helped him realize what it took to reach young people and make them want to learn. He was an excellent communicator.

Alec's gift for communication came in handy at home, too, when dealing with his mother's deafness. Eliza Bell suffered from a serious progressive hearing loss. The family used the manual alphabet at home in order to be able to talk to her, and she benefited somewhat from using an ear trumpet, but somehow she could hear Alec when he spoke in a low tone directly near her forehead. She was a talented painter and pianist who passed her love of music on to all three of her boys. (Alec was a middle child. He and Melly had a younger brother, Ted.) She also taught all of them at home until each boy reached the age of 10. Sadly, she never learned to read lips; this made communication in later years, when she had gone stone deaf, a challenge for her.

Alec inherited his mother's passion for music, and he would play piano while she held her ear trumpet to the instrument to be able to hear the notes. Eliza arranged for Alec to take lessons from a Sr. Auguste Benoit Bertini, one of Edinburgh's most celebrated pianists. Bertini felt the teenager should become a concert pianist. After Bertini's death, Alec gave up on this dream, though he continued to play piano with enthusiasm and grace for the rest of his life. His musical talent and keen ear would stand him in good stead later on, when he was working on his telegraph and other inventions.

Alec's father, Alexander Melville Bell, was devoted to his pursuit of a universal phonetic alphabet, spurred on perhaps by his desire to help Eliza communicate in spite of her deafness. Melville made his living as an elocution instructor, and wrote a bible of sorts for those who wished to speak English properly. Published in 1860, *Bell's Standard Elocutionist* was reprinted over 200 times and was still used over 100 years later as a guide to proper enunciation.

Melville Bell did well as a teacher — though the excellent sales of his books did not quite make his fortune as might have been expected — and was able to buy a nice house in Edinburgh for his family. When Alec was 11, his father purchased a cottage outside of Edinburgh where the family spent at least two days a week from then on. Milton Cottage was the place Alec considered his true boyhood home. Here he spent hours roaming the landscape, collecting specimens for his botany collection, and enjoying the gruff beauty of the Scottish countryside.

In 1864, Melville achieved the culmination of his life's work, a system of symbols that he called "Visible Speech." Each symbol of the Visible Speech alphabet represented a different way of positioning the teeth, tongue, and lips to create a sound (regardless of the language being spoken). He taught all three of his sons to use the system, and they demonstrated it all around Britain at public lectures. Members of the audience would suggest a sound and Melville would transcribe it into the symbols. One of the boys, who had been standing by in another room, would come in and pronounce the sound with remarkable accuracy.

One memorable night, they impressed a scholar of Indian languages: "Prof. Melville Bell, having requested me to test his system of 'Visible Speech' as regards the languages of the East, I selected some of the most difficult words I could think of, in pure Hindoo, Urdu, and Persian ... Students of Oriental languages can only pronounce such words after long practice, and by hearing them uttered by natives of the East. After Mr. Bell had symbolized them on paper, he called in his two sons, who had before that been in a separate room, and asked them to read out the words. To my astonishment, the young men sounded them most accurately, and just as one hears from natives of India."

Melville believed that Visible Speech would be a valuable tool in teaching elocution to hearing people. Alec quickly

Alexander Graham Bell

saw that it could be used as well to teach the deaf to speak. He became one of his father's most enthusiastic supporters, actively promoting and using Visible Speech throughout his life in his work with the deaf.

In fact, Melville Bell's Visible Speech was the precursor to the International Phonetic Alphabet (IPA). The IPA, which is still in use today, is the accepted method of systematic notation for describing the physical gestures by which linguistic (speech) sounds are produced.

Alec once amused himself by teaching his Skye terrier to speak. He managed to teach the dog to growl continuously by bribing him with treats. Then he would manipulate his tongue and vocal chords to produce the following syllables: "Ow ah oo ga ma ma." With only a little prompting, the delighted listener would agree that the dog was saying, "How are you, Grandmamma?" Alec did try to get the dog to speak of his own accord, but noted with disappointment that "he took a bread-and-butter interest in the experiments, but was never able, alone, to do anything but growl."

At the age of 19 Alec began doing his first serious experiments with the transmission of sound in his spare time, using tuning forks to explore resonance. Proud of his discoveries, he wrote them up and sent them off to a colleague of his father's. It turned out that his research followed along the lines of Hermann von Helmholtz, a German scientist who had been working on a similar project with tuning forks. Helmholtz was considered one of the greatest scientists of the 19th century, so Alec was inspired to study the subject further, if a tad disappointed that he hadn't come up with the idea first.

Alec then got hold of the diagrams Helmholtz had made of his tuning fork apparatus, and eagerly pored over them. Helmholtz had managed to create vowel sounds with his contraption. Because Alec didn't really understand how electricity worked, he made a major leap of logic interpreting them, which turned out to be a lucky error for him. "Without knowing much about the subject, it seemed to me," he reflected, "that if vowel sounds could be produced by electrical means so could consonants, so could articulate speech."

From that time on, Alec believed that it would not be long before someone found a way to do this, and he told his friends that the day was coming where they would talk by telegraph. He had no inkling at the time that it would be him — though in his deepest heart he probably dared to dream that it might be. He realized he needed to learn more about electricity if he was to pursue this interest with any chance of advancement.

* * *

One of the greatest losses of Alec's life was about to occur. His younger brother Ted had died in 1867, just a few months short of his 19th birthday. Now, only a few years later, the damp and chill of the Scottish climate had settled in Melly's lungs and he was unable to shake it off. At the age of 25 he succumbed to tuberculosis, the same disease that had claimed Ted's life. Melly had been living in Edinburgh with his young wife, working hard but growing steadily weaker; when Alec went up to see his older brother he was shocked to find him very close to death. The family decided it would be best for Melly to return to London, so he made the journey by train, accompanied by his wife. Alec stayed behind to wrap up his brother's business affairs.

They all still hoped against hope that Melly might recover somehow with a "change of air." But he died only a few days after returning home to London. Alec never got to say a final goodbye to his older brother. His father wrote to him in Edinburgh: "Dear Melly was perfectly conscious of his state, and death had no terrors for him. He expressed himself as glad that he had got home to breathe his last, and we are all thankful on the same account." Melville added poignantly, "Our earthly hopes have now their beginning, middle and end in you."

Alec was now an only child.

He missed his brothers dreadfully. Before Melly died, he and Alec had discussed the possibility of communicating in the afterlife and agreed to give it a try, so he spent some time waiting for a message from Melly from beyond the grave. He didn't hear anything, however, and felt very alone with his uncertain future. He had never been strong as a youth, and he often suffered from debilitating headaches. The spectre of tuberculosis overshadowed his own life, too.

Even before Melly's death, Melville and Eliza had been considering a move to Canada. Now they began to see it as the only way to give their sole remaining child the chance to live a long life. Canada's clean air and wide-open spaces would surely bring Alec back to health. As a youth, Melville had been sent off to Newfoundland for precisely the same reason, and had enjoyed his time there thoroughly, coming back to London totally recovered.

Alec was over 21, though, and just beginning to find his way as an adult in London. He was in love with a woman named Marie Eccleston, who was unlikely to move to the New World with him. He had begun his own teaching career and was making a name for himself, especially as a teacher of the deaf. He was reluctant to give up everything he had going for him in Europe.

However, out of love for his parents he agreed to go. Some accounts of his life say that the move was intended to last only two years as a sort of experiment; however, that seems unlikely, since the Bells sold their house and all their belongings before setting sail.

On July 21, 1870, barely two months after Melly's death, the Bells, along with Melly's widow, Carrie, set out for Ontario. Though in later life he was to travel widely and return fairly frequently to Europe, from the time they arrived, Alec would always call North America home.

Chapter 3
"The Establishment of a Good Profession"

ithin a few weeks of their arrival in Canada, the Bell family bought a house high on the heights above Brantford, overlooking the Grand River. At first, Alec spent his time trying to shake off the illness that had been stalking him at home. He spent his days resting, reading, and thinking. Often he would take himself off to the back of the property, where there was a large hollow amongst the trees above the river. This was his "dreaming place" — and the place where the telephone was eventually conceived.

But in the summer of 1870, other thoughts occupied Alec as he watched the river moving below him and the clouds passing overhead. He was not very sick with tuberculosis, but neither was he a strong young man. He wondered if he would survive, even now that he was in Canada where the air was fresh and clean. Being Alec, he also thought about electricity and sound. There were so many things he wanted to learn, to study, and to invent. He never was one for lazing around.

Bit by bit, the sunshine and healthy air of Canada began to do their work. Alec regained his colour and his zest for life. He spent some time on the Six Nations Reserve across the river, learning Mohawk and translating their language into Visible Speech. For this work, he was granted the title of honourary chief, and was photographed wearing the ceremonial regalia of the tribe. He even learned their war dance which, for the rest of his life, he executed when he was very excited.

He may well have done this dance when he received a letter from the Horace Mann School for the Deaf early in 1871. The principal, Sarah Fuller, had heard about Alec's novel methods for teaching the deaf to speak. Would he be interested — "for a handsome appropriation" — in travelling to Boston to teach the deaf-mute children at her school, and to train their teachers in the use of Visible Speech?

He was more than interested. Within two weeks, he was on a train for Boston.

Alec was a patient teacher who built up his students' confidence bit by bit, and his novel methods rapidly bore fruit for these previously silent children. Within a few weeks of his arrival, the children were making hundreds of sounds that they had never been able to produce before. From this summer on, he considered his most important job to be teaching the deaf to speak.

After the Horace Mann School, he taught at several other schools for the deaf in New England. Everywhere he taught, especially when teaching children, he encountered the same type of results as he had at the Boston school. Clearly, the techniques he was using were winners.

* * *

"October 1, 1872. Master George Sanders, aged 5 years, became my pupil this morning. He was born totally deaf; and has never spoken a word in his life ... He seems a fine, bright, intelligent boy; and there is no apparent defect in his vocal organs ..."

Georgie Sanders came to Alec on the recommendation of Sarah Fuller. This recommendation was to change Alec's life as irrevocably as it did Georgie's, but for very different reasons.

Like so many of Alec's pupils, Georgie made excellent and rapid progress. Before he turned six he had learned to read and write, and could communicate with Alec by spelling out words on a special glove Alec had designed for the purpose. Thanks to Alec, the world had opened up for Georgie in ways in which his wealthy father, Thomas Sanders, had never dared to hope.

"The Establishment of a Good Profession"

Alec eventually moved into Georgie's grandmother's spacious house in Salem, near Boston. For the perpetually cash-strapped young teacher, earning room and board as well as tuition fees in exchange for instructing Georgie was a godsend. He grew very close to Mrs. Sanders and saw her as a sort of surrogate mother.

Buoyed by his work with Georgie, Alec began to take on more deaf students. While his students made great progress, he realized that he alone could not teach every deaf child to speak. He had to get more teachers involved in the Visible Speech method, and to that end he opened his own school in Boston: the School of Vocal Physiology and Mechanics of Speech.

Alec's students — both the children he taught directly and the teachers he trained in Visible Speech — were very important to him. He had a true gift for teaching, for unlocking the silent world of the deaf and allowing them to communicate more easily with hearing people. More prosaically, these students were his only source of regular income. He was committed to keeping this vocation of his going.

But he had another passion, just as compelling: the urge to invent.

He had to teach during the day, so at night and on weekends he would work away in secret on his various contraptions. Mrs. Sanders helped him out by allowing him the use of her cellar and, later on, her third floor for his workshop. This was another relief to Alec, who constantly feared someone would steal his work.

His main goal at first was to use new technology in order to create new and better ways of teaching the deaf to speak. But as he worked away, he began to see other inventions that would have much broader uses. He began to think about a device he called the "harmonic telegraph" or multiple telegraph.

In those days, the telegraph was very expensive for the average person to use, so it was primarily used by businesses. By the 1870s, there was essentially a monopoly on the telegraph wires. One very large company dominated the entire industry: Western Union. The company completed the transcontinental telegraph line in 1861 and within a few years controlled about 90 percent of all telegraph messages sent in the United States.

The limitations of telegraph technology were becoming apparent already. Only one message at a time could travel over the wires, which led to backlogs and delays in getting messages through. The first inventor to come up with a good way to send more than one message over the same line was going to become very wealthy. Several well-known inventors — and others not so well known — had their sights set on this prize.

Alec joined their ranks when he started making designs for his harmonic telegraph in 1872. The race was on.

At 25, he wanted to find a way to become financially stable so he would be a good marriage prospect. Of course, he was also ambitious and eager to make his mark in the world. His whole life he had felt somewhat in awe of his father's achievements. If Alec could make one solid invention, his own place in the world would be assured. Little did he know his name would become so famous that he and his work would completely overshadow even the impressive accomplishments of his father.

After only a few months of work, Alec had devised a machine that would transmit two messages simultaneously. This was excellent progress for a part-time inventor with no formal training in the ways of electricity. But Joseph Stearns, another inventor, had beaten him to this stage — and Western Union had already snapped up his "duplex telegraph."

The basic concept behind Alec's harmonic telegraph was that many messages could be sent through one wire if each message was sent at a different pitch, to be picked up at the other end by a receiver tuned to the same pitch. He kept working away in secret to perfect his apparatus, which consisted of various tuning forks set to different pitches, all powered by a battery.

He stretched himself to the limit: teaching and grading papers, giving public lectures about Visible Speech, and working on telegraphy through many long nights. Since he had little money, he strained himself financially, too, in order to pay for supplies for his inventing. He often worked so hard he made himself physically ill, suffering from terrible, protracted headaches. Fortunately, he had Brantford to return to.

Every summer, he would go home for at least a month to rest and restore his energy.

On August 10, 1874, Alec reclined in his "dreaming place" above the Grand River and thought about electricity, magnets and circuits, tuning forks and speech. And it was here that he had the most enormous thought of his life. Probably it was a hot and sultry day, as it usually is in Ontario in August. Alec was thinking about how sound travels through the air, in waves. "I wonder," he thought, "if the vibrations of the voice might create electrical impulses like the aerial impulses, and produce an audible result at the other end."

He later reminisced about this moment. "To tell you the truth, as a practical man, I did not quite believe it ... it really seemed too good to be true."

With the help of his friend Clarence Blake, a doctor, Alec devised a machine called a "phonautograph." It consisted of a human ear (which Blake obtained from a cadaver and mailed to Alec) with the eardrum attached to a stylus above a piece of glass. Alec would speak into the ear and watch as his words turned into tracings on glass. He thought that providing an image of sound waves would give his students visible feedback on their speech mechanics, thereby helping them to speak more clearly.

Eventually Alec discovered that the phonautograph was not going to be a useful tool for his deaf students, but the experiment was very important anyway, for it showed Alec that sound does indeed travel in an undulating current. Now all he had to do was solve a bit more of the puzzle in order to create that current. But it would be some time before all those pieces fell together. And Alec had other things on his mind.

Chapter 4
"I Thought Alone of You, Mabel"

n the summer of 1874, while Alec was thinking about electricity, sound waves, undulating currents, and other weighty topics, his mind wandered off at times to linger on thoughts of a young lady named Mabel Hubbard. He scarcely dared to admit it to himself at this point, but the serious young Alexander Graham Bell was smitten.

Mabel had entered Alec's life in 1873, when he became her teacher. She had not heard a thing in more than a decade, after an attack of scarlet fever at the age of five left her totally deaf. By the time she met Alec, she was an educated young lady of not quite 16, with clear blue eyes and a sharp mind. Her story in itself is rather remarkable.

In 1862, as the little girl began to recover from her fever, it became apparent to Mabel's parents that their daughter's hearing was gone. There was nothing wrong with her brain or her vocal chords, but her future seemed very bleak indeed. Since she could no longer hear herself speak, she would gradually lose the power of language.

Experts at the time recommended that the deaf learn to use sign language. Deaf children were sent to asylums (residential schools) where everyone spoke with signs and no speech was ever used. Worse still, a child had to be 10 years old before even being considered for a place at one of these schools. Following traditional wisdom, this bright little girl would spend five years in silence — unteachable, unreachable — before she could even think of going to school.

Luckily for Mabel, she had been born to a pair of very strong-minded parents. They refused to accept that their beloved daughter would have to be different from her sisters, or from the rest of the world. If she couldn't hear, she was still going to speak.

Mabel's father was Gardiner Greene Hubbard, a wealthy Boston patent lawyer. He and his wife, Gertrude, decided that Mabel would learn to read lips and would continue to speak. She would not be taught sign language. She would not be allowed to communicate through gestures or miming. What Gardiner and Gertrude were doing for Mabel flew in the face of all the accepted wisdom about the deaf in that era, but they were convinced it was their daughter's only chance for a normal life.

Most parents would have tried to do the best they could for their own daughter, but Hubbard went several steps further. He was a philanthropist and a persuasive speaker who rarely shrank from a challenge. In 1864 he petitioned the Massachusetts State Legislature to set up a state school for children like Mabel, where they could learn to read lips and to speak using the so-called "oral method" of educating the deaf, which was being taught in some places in Europe. By this time, Mabel was making great educational progress at home, learning through this method from an excellent teacher named Mary True.

Hubbard was unable to get a state school going in his first attempt. Undaunted, a few years later he set up a small private school for the deaf where the oral method was the very successful standard. But only a few years later on, he was back in front of the legislature, with the same request for public schooling for deaf children. And this time he brought Mabel with him.

Amazingly, at nine years old Mabel had no idea she was any different from other people. Thanks to the determination and love of her family and Mary True, she was an able lip reader and was well ahead of her age in most school subjects.

The committee of the legislature examined Mabel, asking her questions to test her education. At first they could not believe that she was not able to hear, such was her facility with lip reading. Her voice sounded a little odd, but was perfectly intelligible. She was a shining example of how well a deaf person could succeed in ordinary society by using the oral method.

Mabel's convincing performance as a witness was one of the major factors in the Legislature's decision to open a state school for the deaf, as her father so dearly wished. The Clarke Institution for Deaf Mutes (named after the man who first put up the money for it) opened in 1867 in Northampton, Massachusetts. It is still in operation today.

The Hubbards departed for Europe a few years later so Mabel could attend school in Germany. Despite her deafness, Mabel became totally fluent in German. However, the school she attended was not specially aimed at the deaf, so her speech didn't improve noticeably during that time.

In 1873 they returned home to Boston to meet with Professor Alexander Graham Bell, who had developed a reputation in Boston as a wonderful teacher of deaf children. Gardiner Greene Hubbard, who had remained closely involved with the Clarke School after it was set up, had met Alec there briefly a year earlier. It was time for Mabel to benefit from Alec's expertise as a teacher.

Mary True, who had become a teacher in the Horace Mann School for the Deaf, took Mabel to her first meeting with Alec. At the time, Mabel saw improving her speech as a way to increase her chances of acquiring a rich husband, perhaps a lawyer like her father, and to be comfortable in the Boston society of which she would undoubtedly be a part.

Despite Mary's assurances that working with Professor Bell would be well worth her while, Mabel went along to her first lesson privately fearing Alec would turn out to be some kind of quack doctor.

It was not love at first sight for either one of them. Alec undoubtedly saw Mabel as just a young girl at first, another of his deaf students, but not in any way remarkable except for her family connections.

For her part, Mabel was dismayed by her teacher's rather frumpy appearance and assumed he must be at least in his mid-thirties (he was 26). As she confided to her diary that night, "Altogether, I do not think him exactly a gentleman ... *I* could never marry such a man." While Mabel was a very bright and well-mannered young woman, we must not forget that she was still just a teenager who probably spent a lot of time thinking about cute boys. Alec was neither cute nor a boy. He was intense and serious. He was her teacher.

But what a teacher he was. He engaged Mabel in a way that no other teacher had ever done before. She found him "so quick, so enthusiastic, so compelling, I had whether I would or no to follow all he said and tax my brains to respond as he desired."

So it was a blow to Mabel when she arrived for her lesson one day to discover that he had passed on his teaching duties to his assistant, Abby Locke. Mabel was blissfully unaware that Alec was beginning to fall for her. Alec managed to conceal his growing passion from her parents, and even from himself, for quite some time. But he could not go on teaching her — such an arrangement would have been most improper, even if Mabel remained ignorant of his feelings.

When Alec was not teaching or working on his inventions, he often dropped in to visit the Hubbard household on a Sunday afternoon. Mabel and her sisters were lively company, and Gardiner and Gertrude had developed an affection and respect for their daughter's teacher. For this penniless young man, the Hubbard mansion on Brattle Street must have seemed a warm and welcoming place. It was furnished expensively but comfortably, with plenty of books and a piano that was a big draw for the music lover in Alec. He played the piano, enjoyed a meal, and chatted with the family. In summer, they spent time in the garden. Every moment of being near Mabel was a pleasure for Alec.

In June 1875, Mabel made plans to spend the summer on Nantucket Island with her cousin, Mary Blatchford. When he heard the news, Alec felt completely shocked. He realized he couldn't bear to think that he would not see Mabel for the whole summer. He finally had to admit to himself that he was in love with his young student. After some thought, he decided to proclaim his love for her. He professed it not directly to her — that would have been most improper — but to her mother. (Normally he would have gone to her father, but Gardiner Greene Hubbard was away at the time for an indefinite period, and the impetuous suitor felt he couldn't wait another moment.)

"I am in deep trouble and can only go to you for advice," he wrote. "I have discovered that my interest in my dear pupil, Mabel, has ripened into a far deeper feeling than that of mere friendship. In fact I know that I have learned to love her very sincerely ... It is my desire to let her know — now — how dear she has become to me, and to ascertain from her own lips what her feeling towards me may be."

He knew Gertrude might be alarmed at his boldness, and he was a man of honour, so he assured her he would follow her wishes. "I promise beforehand to abide by your decision, however hard it may be for me to do so." Mrs. Hubbard asked Alec to wait a year before telling Mabel how he felt, and he reluctantly promised to do so. When Gardiner Greene Hubbard returned from his trip, he backed up his wife's decision, telling the young man he would have preferred a *two*-year wait before allowing Mabel to be informed of Alec's hopes.

The Hubbards were unwilling to allow Mabel to be courted by a man so much older. They, too, had thought Alec to be much older than his 26 years, and they still felt a significant age gap existed between their daughter and her teacher. At only 17, Mabel should be given the opportunity to "enter into society — and meet with others — before asking her to decide one way or the other."

Alec did his best to keep his feelings to himself, but within a month he was ready to burst. He told the Hubbards he had to tell Mabel how he felt; he believed she should know the truth. They asked him to be patient and wait a while longer since, as he wrote glumly in his journal, "they feared Mabel would be startled and distressed" at his declaration.

He wrote to Mrs. Hubbard several times over the course of the summer, and she began to act as intermediary between her daughter and Alec. By early August he could wait no longer. He set out for Nantucket, valise in hand, to meet with Mabel. He told the Hubbards that he had to go, being "ill — further delay and anxiety would entirely unfit me for anything."

He finally arrived at Nantucket and encountered an extraordinary rainstorm that rendered the road to the place where Mabel was staying an impassable mud bog. It seemed like everything was conspiring against him. He felt unwell, with a nervous headache, and was unable to sleep. He decided to write Mabel a letter instead of going to see her. It turned into a lengthy and impassioned plea, explaining all that had been in his heart all summer long, when *"I thought alone of you, Mabel."*

He wrote: "I have loved you with a passionate attachment that you cannot understand and that is to myself — new — and incomprehensible. I wished to tell you of my wish to make you my wife — if you would let me try to win your love."

At the end of the letter he wrote, "I do not want to commit you to any course of action ... I merely wish that you should know my *heart* — and then I feel that I can leave you with the consciousness of having been true to myself — and just to you — and leave all else to time."

He had only one request of Mabel. "Tell me frankly all that there is in me that you dislike and that I can alter."

The next morning he made the trip out to where Mabel was staying, but her cousin Mary Blatchford told him Mabel would not see him, so he didn't push, but went home to Boston, where he stopped in at the Hubbards' to tell them what had happened. Tired, but happy that he had finally told the truth, he wrote in his journal, "Even Mr. Hubbard admitted that I had done well." Then he went home and slept for the first time in 10 days.

He and Mabel began to correspond as friends, and she assured him that he had both her "respect and esteem." In only a few months' time Alec wrote to the Hubbards again, telling them that he intended to woo Mabel if she seemed responsive. "When I am *sure of her affections* I wish to be engaged to her — when I am in a position to offer her a home I wish to *marry* her — whether it be in two years or two months!"

To Alec's joy, Mrs. Hubbard replied, "I give you back your promise, entirely, unreservedly. I believe your love to my Mabel to be unselfish and noble. I trust you perfectly. If you can win her love I shall feel happy in my darling's happiness."

He went to the Hubbards' the next day and spent time alone with Mabel. While she told him she didn't love him, she encouraged him to continue seeing her. Later on that night, he wrote jubilantly in his diary, "*The happiest day of my life* ...

Shall not write any more here. I feel that I have at last got to the end of all my troubles."

Chapter 5
"It Is a Neck and Neck Race"

or years, Alec struggled to find a financial backer for his research. "I have invented a method by which a large number of telegraphic messages can be sent along the same wire, at the same time, without confusing with one another," Alec wrote in January 1874. He was trying to get the British government interested in buying his invention. In no time flat, he received a chilly refusal from London.

So when he made a similar comment to Gardiner Greene Hubbard in October that same year, he was ecstatic at Hubbard's response. Alec wrote shortly afterwards that "he now offers to provide me with *funds* for the purpose of experimenting if we go into the scheme as partners ... You will understand what an encouragement this is to me. To find that the man who is the head of the Telegraphic Systems of the States is willing to become a partner in the development of the scheme gives me greater confidence in my own ideas."

For his part, Hubbard was stunned and delighted to hear Alec's news, since for several years he had been lobbying Congress for a charter to operate a company that would rival Western Union. He felt passionately that it was wrong for one private company to have such a monopoly. Moreover, he believed there were good profits to be made in telegraphy, plenty for two companies and many more. He wanted part of those profits, and he thought that the multiple telegraph provided the way to compete with Western Union.

Alec could hardly believe his good fortune. Only a few days earlier, Thomas Sanders (Georgie's father) had offered to back him. Now he had Hubbard on his side as well.

He went back to Sanders and told him about Hubbard's interest. Nervously, Sanders said, "I think it was unwise to have told the idea to Mr. Hubbard. Public men are so corrupt, and the idea will be worth thousands of dollars to Mr. Hubbard." He urged Alec to get a patent as soon as possible, to protect himself in case Hubbard had designs on taking Alec's idea. But despite Sanders's initial misgivings about Hubbard, both men had faith in Alec and in his invention; before long, they had both agreed to back Alec financially.

While Hubbard ultimately proved himself to be a man of integrity and honour, Sanders's suggestion that Alec acquire a patent was sound advice. A patent would provide protection from other inventors and from people who really did wish to steal his ideas. Alec put the wheels in motion to apply for American citizenship, so he could take out a caveat if he needed to.

A caveat was a precursor to a patent. It was a statement of an intention to invent something — the one filing the caveat would explain his basic concept to the patent office, to protect it in case someone else came up with a similar idea while the inventor continued working on it. Once a caveat was registered, its holder was considered to have priority on the idea. If another inventor then tried to register a similar caveat, he would be turned down. This, of course, would tip the second inventor off that he might be onto something, even though the details of the first caveat were never made public.

A certain caveat was to play an important role in the future of the telephone, but this was still months in the future. Now, Alec and his two backers signed a simple agreement. The three of them would split equally any proceeds from the young man's telegraphic inventions.

Alec had finally found his backers.

According to their agreement, Alec would be reimbursed for any expenses incurred in building and perfecting the machine. He could also hire a helper whose salary would be paid by Sanders. Alec himself was not put on any salary, which undoubtedly sharpened his desire to get the apparatus running well enough to be sold for a handsome fee.

He became busier than ever. He still had to keep his teaching commitments, especially to the private pupils who were his main source of income. But he really had to put more time into the multiple telegraph development, to keep up his end of the bargain with Sanders and Hubbard. He fell back into his old habits of working ridiculously long hours in an effort to make everything go smoothly.

Alec faced serious competition. In a letter to his parents, he commented, "It is a neck and neck race between Mr. Gray and myself who shall complete our apparatus first. He has the advantage over me of being a practical electrician — but I have reason to believe that I am better acquainted with the phenomenon of sound than he is." Alec felt energized by the competition with Gray and worked hard to keep ahead of him.

However, Alec's mind was filled with thoughts of going further, of creating a machine that would transmit speech. That summer in Brantford he had come up with the idea, and he was anxious to pursue it further. He had checked his theory out with a respected electrician he knew, who had said it *should* work, but Alec felt it was still years away from being put into practice. He was anxious to get to work on this intriguing new device. In fact, in the very same letter to his parents in which he wrote about his rivalry with Gray, he mentioned the principle of the telephone, "an instrument by which the human voice might be telegraphed *without the use of a battery at all.*" He explained that when a permanent magnet is made to vibrate in front of an electromagnet, the vibrations will create an electrical vibration in the live wire and will force vibration in the receiving apparatus (he envisioned it looking like a harp, so for the time being he called it his "harp apparatus").

Though he was cautious to a fault about maintaining secrecy, Alec would occasionally seek help in building his machines. He had plenty of vision for design, but often needed a more skilled person to bring a design to life. Also, he was never sure of his own electrical knowledge and needed to consult with those who knew more than he did. He trusted few people, but those he did usually came through for him, offering advice and encouragement when the young inventor needed it most.

He began to frequent Charles Williams's shop in Boston. In this remarkable workshop, young electrical engineers — then called "electricians" — worked to turn out electrical supplies and to build designs for hopeful inventors. Working with hand lathes, or using simple vises and files, these electricians had a hand in some of the most interesting work going on in the country. They built designs for Alec, Thomas Edison, Elisha Gray, and many other talented inventors of the day.

It was here that Alec met one of his most helpful allies, Thomas A. Watson. Watson was a gifted electrician who worked on various projects in the Williams shop. He had had several jobs before coming to work for Williams, and indeed, after working on the telephone, went on to many other achievements. By 1901, he would have built a small shipbuilding concern into the largest shipyard in the United States. Still later, he went on to become an actor and playwright. But when he and Alec met, he was still one of Charles Williams's employees. His passion was electricity — he read everything he could find about the subject. He was also very handy and could knock together Alec's designs overnight. Without Watson at his side, it is quite possible that Alec would not have been able to invent the telephone.

Sanders and Hubbard were thankful when Thomas Watson entered the picture. It drove them crazy when Alec went off on tangents like this harp apparatus idea of his, so they hoped an assistant would keep him focused. Once their enthusiastic young inventor got the multiple telegraph working, they felt, he would have the money and the leisure to dabble in any other invention he pleased.

In January 1875, Thomas Watson became Alec's full-time assistant, little knowing that his name would go down in history. The two young men became friends over the long hours they put in, trying to perfect the multiple telegraph in their laboratory above Charles Williams's Boston shop. Watson suggested numerous adaptations to Alec's original idea until they had a machine they were confident would be able to send 30 to 40 messages at a time over the same wire. It was time to apply for a patent.

Alec set off for Washington with his multiple telegraph and applied for three patents to protect his work on the machine. To his surprise, Elisha Gray applied for a patent in the very same week, on *his* multiple telegraph. Despite the ideal that each inventor's privacy should be scrupulously guarded, the patent business in Washington was a small community and rumours obviously circulated. It's not clear whether Gray's patent lawyer had an informant, but certainly his patent applications often seemed to coincide rather eerily with Alec's.

The two competing applications posed a problem to the patent office, so neither inventor was permitted to go further until the matter was sorted out. Months went by before the patent officer ruled that two of Alec's applications interfered with Gray's application, which effectively killed both inventors' patents. Alec's third patent application, for a telautograph (a sort of early fax machine) was eventually granted.

On a cold, blustery March day, Alec entered the doors of the Smithsonian Institution in search of encouragement. He had arranged a meeting with Smithsonian director Joseph Henry. Henry, then close to 80 years old, had an impeccable reputation as a scientist and electrician. A generation earlier he had come very close to inventing the telegraph, but Samuel Morse had taken Henry's published ideas further and had subsequently gone down in history as the inventor of that very useful communication method.

While the main purpose of Alec's visit to the Smithsonian was to show its director the multiple telegraph, he also intended to pluck up the courage to ask Henry for advice about his most cherished new idea, the harp apparatus.

Despite the chilly day, Henry's welcome was warm. He became very excited when Alec told him about his idea of transmitting speech over wires without a battery. He listened carefully as Alec explained how he thought it could work.

"What would you advise me to do — publish the idea and let others work it out, or attempt to solve the problem myself?" asked Alec anxiously.

"I think you have the germ of a great invention. I advise you to work at it yourself instead of publishing it," replied Henry, doubtless thinking of how his life might have been different had someone given him that advice years earlier.

Alec was still uncertain. He knew there were many potential obstacles and problems, and he told Henry, "I feel I don't have the electrical knowledge necessary to overcome the difficulties."

Henry's answer was succinct: *"Get it!"*

Alec took heart. He had faith in his new idea but his partners were much more interested in the multiple telegraph. To have such an eminent scientist as Joseph Henry enthusiastically supporting him made him feel confident he would succeed. With typical overstatement, he wrote to his parents, "My visit to the Smithsonian Institute seems to be the brightest spot in my whole life. I feel now that I am accepted by scientific men as one of themselves."

Full of hope, he set off for his next meeting in New

York City. This time he was up against a more formidable person — William Orton, the president of Western Union and one of the most powerful men in America. Upon seeing a preliminary demonstration of Alec's multiple telegraph in Washington, Orton invited Alec to Western Union's head office for further trials. When he issued his invitation, Orton told Alec, "The Western Union would be glad to give you every facility in perfecting your instruments." Excitedly, Alec wrote to his parents that, in addition, Orton "wished me distinctly to understand that the Western Union had no interest in Mr. Gray or his invention."

The test transmission of multiple messages over 200 miles of telegraph wire was an unqualified success. Even Alec was surprised at how well his machine worked, since the batteries he was using were only intended for use over shorter lengths of wire. "The signals, though feeble, came sharply and concisely through the 200 miles of live-wire!!!"

The electrician for Western Union took the machine off to their workshop, telling Alec it would be fitted with stronger magnets for a repeat test that afternoon. Alec was jubilant as he headed out of the Western Union headquarters for lunch. He felt that Orton had been really impressed with how the machine sent multiple messages. Maybe the big man would offer to buy the apparatus right then and there.

When he returned that afternoon, he spent a long time with Western Union's electricians explaining exactly how the machine worked. Then he met again with Orton. He was shocked to discover that the president of Western Union had completely changed his tune in only a few hours. Orton explained that, in another one of those odd coincidences, Elisha Gray had dropped by to call on Orton while Alec was at lunch. Although inwardly furious, Alec kept a calm outer demeanour as Orton told him he felt Elisha Gray's apparatus was the better one.

Orton then told Alec, "The Western Union will never take up a scheme which will benefit Mr. Hubbard." He had a long memory and was not about to forgive Gardiner Greene Hubbard for his repeated attempts to break Western Union's telegraphic monopoly.

Alec's anxiety and anger peaked as he realized Western Union had "tried to get as much information out of me as possible — and then at the last minute had turned me off."

He contacted Hubbard right away for advice. "I do not wish to stand in your way," Hubbard said, "so I will withdraw if the Western Union would be inclined to come to terms with you personally." Alec, of course, would not hear of it. Hubbard then advised him to go back to Western Union the very next day, to retrieve his machine and confront Orton.

Orton, however, was a practiced manipulator. When Alec returned the next morning to pick up his machine, Orton told him there was still a chance Western Union would buy his multiple telegraph once it was perfected, even if Hubbard *was* involved. But he wanted Hubbard to take all the risk; he would only step in and buy the working machine once all the bugs had been worked out. "I can hardly think that you have treated me fairly," Alec said — mildly, under the circumstances. He threatened to take his machine directly across the street to Western Union's rival telegraph company, but Orton was prepared for this threat and serenely replied, "If you take your invention to the Atlantic and Pacific Corp., we shall at once take up Gray."

Alec had been outmanoeuvred.

Being a proud man of considerable integrity, Alec doubtless wished to tell the arrogant and insincere Orton where to go, but he needed his machine to be a winner. Sanders and Hubbard had already put their money and support into the scheme. Alec was tired of being broke all the time. If Orton had offered to buy the rights to Alec's invention, he probably would have jumped at the chance to sell them. But Orton didn't. What should have been a triumphant moment for Alec had instead created aggravation and worry for the young inventor.

An exhausted Alec returned to Boston and took to his bed for several days, recovering from one of his sick headaches. When he felt well again, he cancelled most of his teaching commitments and worked almost exclusively on his multiple telegraph. He had to make it work. He was too proud to ask Hubbard for more money. The months dragged by and he was beginning to be sick of the whole thing. Would it never be perfected?

And then, one muggy day in early June, a most astonishing thing happened. Alec and Watson were working on the multiple telegraph in their lab above Charles Williams's shop. They had rigged wires to run from one room to the next and were trying to send three signals at once. The reeds they were working with were slim strips of metal that would sound a specific tone when plucked, each at a different frequency. They were fiddly to work with, and one got stuck on Watson's transmitter. He turned off the battery and plucked at the reed several times to free it.

Alec, working 20 metres away in the other room, heard the twang on his receiver. He ran down the hall and demanded to see what Watson had done. Watson showed him, and the two men looked at each other for a long moment. Both realized the importance of what had happened. The reeds had generated an undulatory current exactly as Alec had theorized the summer before. This meant that sound really *could* induce a current, travel through a wire electrically, and come out again as sound at the other end of the wire.

Alec's theory of the telephone was right.

He wrote to Gardiner Greene Hubbard that very night, saying, "I have accidentally made a discovery of the very greatest importance ... I have succeeded today in transmitting signals *without any battery whatever!"*

Alec and Watson immediately began work on a new machine, based on Alec's idea from the summer before of a "membrane telephone." Within a few days it was ready for testing, and shortly afterwards, Watson heard Alec's sonorous voice through the wire. Alec could not hear Watson when the tables were turned, however, perhaps because Watson lacked Alec's elocutionary skills. Still, they knew they were onto something big.

That summer was not very productive in terms of the invention. Alec was caught up in the passion and confusion of his pursuit of Mabel, and Watson suffered from a bout of typhoid. The machine sat idle for a couple of months. But once Alec had come clean about his love for Mabel and had not been rejected, it was as if a great weight had been lifted from his shoulders. In the fall of 1875 he shook off the fog of emotions that had surrounded him for months. Now he had a most pressing need to get his inventions going — he planned to propose to Mabel as soon as he felt financially stable.

He got back to work in earnest, placing most of his other commitments on hold so he could get his patent application going. He began to write it up in his old room at Tutelo Heights, when he returned home to Brantford for a holiday. The application for "improvements in telegraphy" was very detailed and, although it did not mention the telephone as a separate device, it included Alec's theory of speech transmission.

As Alec worked on his patent application, he clashed with Gardiner Greene Hubbard several times. Hubbard was still most anxious for Alec to get his harmonic telegraph in commercial working order. He felt that Alec was spending far too much time on his students and on this distracting toy he called the telephone.

He scolded Alec for his lack of focus, and the "tendency of your mind to undertake every new thing that interests you and accomplish nothing of any value to anyone." At one point, utterly frustrated by Alec's seeming commitment to everything but the multiple telegraph, Hubbard even tried to use his daughter's hand as a bargaining chip: either Alec could finish his telegraph and continue to court her, or he could just go back to being a teacher of the deaf who dabbled in inventing. If he did the latter, he could forget about his dream of marrying Mabel.

Alec was incensed at this ultimatum, but his reply to Gardiner Hubbard was reasoned. He pointed out that he was actually making a decent living as a teacher and professor. "Should Mabel learn to love me as devotedly and truly as I do her — she will not object to any work in which I may be engaged so long as it is honourable and profitable. If she does not come to love me well enough to accept me *whatever my profession or business may be* — I do not want her at all. I do not want a half-love — nor do I want her to marry my *profession!*" He asked Hubbard to bear with him a little longer.

In the end Hubbard's ultimatum had the opposite effect from what he had intended. Mabel no longer wished to be caught in the middle of her father and Alec, and on her 18th birthday, which was also Thanksgiving Day, she told Alec she loved him and would be his wife. He was overwhelmingly happy. (It was at this time — in response to Mabel's request, and perhaps to underline his newly engaged state — that he began to spell his name "Alec" rather than "Aleck.")

It seemed like everything was going right for Alec. He felt optimistic about his love life, his health, his teaching, and his telegraphy. All he needed was the money to file his patent applications in the United States, and in other countries, as soon as possible. His agreement with Hubbard and Sanders only covered American patents and profits. He felt he had already asked enough of these two generous men. What he really wanted was to find another backer to help him with patent applications in other countries. And so George Brown, a well-to-do neighbour from Brantford, entered the picture.

The formidable Brown, founder of the Toronto *Globe*, had been actively involved in Canadian national politics for many years. Now he was advanced in years. He enjoyed his large hobby farm and his considerable wealth, and continued to write fiery editorials for the *Globe* and to follow politics with a keen interest. He met with Alec in the fall of 1875, when Alec was home in Brantford for a visit with his parents. Brown and his brother eventually agreed to help Alec by financing his work and filing for the patents. They must have felt they were doing their neighbour a big favour. Their agreement ran as follows: "We hereby agree to pay you twenty-five dollars in U.S. currency each of us per month while you are perfecting your improvements in telegraphy and preparing the necessary specifications for taking out patents ... said monthly payments to cease when the patents are obtained and in no case to extend beyond six months."

"It Is a Neck and Neck Race"

Though Alec and the Brown brothers could not know it at the time, this was possibly the best deal in history. In return for $300, Alec promised to give each brother one quarter of any profits from the patent in the British Empire (including Canada). He also gave them a dangerous level of control over his own invention — he agreed to hold off on applying for an American patent until the British patent had been granted.

Alec waited impatiently for the first month's money to arrive. He had found a new teacher for Georgie Sanders and had moved out of the house in Salem; he now needed to pay rent on his new rooms in Exeter Place, Boston. But no cheque arrived.

He finally received $50 from the Browns in January, just before George Brown set sail for England to file the patents there. Alec had no inkling that he had made a major oversight in his English patent application. He did not include a certain vital specification, relating to the variable resistance transmission of speech, which had been included in the US patent application.

Brown was supposed to file the papers as soon as he arrived in Britain, then send word to an anxious Alec waiting in Boston. As Hubbard put it in a letter to Alec, "There is now much excitement in this branch of Telegraphy ... the specification should be filed as soon as possible." However, Alec's American patent lawyers had to wait until the British one was filed, due to Alec's agreement with the Browns. The wait dragged on for days, then weeks. Every day that Alec delayed his application was a day that someone else might beat him to it, and then all his work would have been for naught.

Finally, in late February, Brown told Alec that he had showed the multiple telegraph application to several noted British scientists and electricians, who had told him it was worthless. The crucial clause was missing that would have made the application valid, so he hadn't even bothered to file the application. He was no longer interested in working with Alec.

Brown never even discussed the telephone with anyone in England. Fortunately, by then it didn't matter. Gardiner Greene Hubbard had become tired of waiting, and had filed the application (without Alec's knowledge) on February 14, 1876.

Alec was angry when he found out what Hubbard had done. Despite the fact that George Brown had not upheld his part of the bargain, Alec's integrity was so strong that he still felt compelled to keep his promise to Brown. However, Alec was soon to thank his lucky stars that Hubbard had acted when he did. On the very same day that Alec's application was filed, only a few hours later, Elisha Gray filed a caveat for a telephone.

Both applications were suspended as the Patent Office tried to sort out who had precedence. Alec stopped in at the patent office and met with the man in charge of issuing patents, Zenas Wilber. He spent some time explaining his invention and how it worked. After his meeting with Wilber,

Alec felt that "he must have been convinced of my independent conception of the whole thing." Besides, Alec could produce a working machine — something Gray was unable to do. All Gray had done was to come up with an idea that might someday become a reality.

Alec waited impatiently in Washington for news of his application. He wrote to his father in the meantime. "I am sure of fame, fortune and success if I can only persevere in perfecting my apparatus." But he didn't know if he could overcome the interference that Gray's caveat had produced. Until the patent was actually issued, Alec couldn't count on anything.

Finally, on his 29th birthday, Alec received the best possible gift — news that his patent would be granted. Patent No. 174,465 was issued a few days later, and went on to become one of the most valuable patents in history.

However, Alec still had work to do. He and Watson got right back to their experiments in Boston, trying to make the telephone a working reality.

On March 10, 1876, just three days after the telephone patent was issued, one of his most cherished dreams came true. He and Watson were working in the lab at Exeter Place, constantly refining, changing, and testing their design. That day they were testing a new type of liquid variable-resistance transmitter, which involved battery acid in a dish. Alec was at the transmitter, Watson at the receiver in a room at the end of the hall. Alec shouted to Watson, "Mr. Watson — come here

— I want to see you."

Watson came running, his face alight with joy. He had heard Alec's voice clearly *through the receiver*. All their hard work had finally come together with those few words.

They switched places, and Watson sang a tune, then read a few passages from a book so Alec could hear at the other end. As Alec wrote to his father, Watson's "voice came from the electro-magnet in a curious half-muffled sort of a way." He could make out words here and there, but not the entire passage. Finally Watson ended by enquiring, very clearly, "Mr. Bell, do you understand what I say?"

Alec understood, indeed. The afternoon was to have an enormous impact on his life, and on the entire world. As he wrote later that evening, "the day is coming when telegraph wires will be laid on to houses just like water or gas — and friends converse with each other without leaving home." It was the dawn of an entirely new era in communication.

Alec and Watson kept on testing the telephone throughout the day, singing to each other, reading passages from books, and shouting. The sound was not exceptionally clear, and the conversation was at this time only one-way. There was still plenty of work to be done before the machine would be commercially functional.

Over the next few months, Alec and Watson continued to modify and perfect the apparatus. Hubbard was now convinced that the telephone had possibilities, but he continued to press Alec just to finish one thing — the multiple telegraph — before rushing headlong into the Next Big Thing. However, Hubbard did participate in several tests of the telephone, some quite successful. Once the machine appeared to be working fairly reliably, Hubbard began to encourage Alec to exhibit the telephone at the Centennial Exhibition in Philadelphia.

It was time for Alec's invention to be introduced to the world.

With the dramatic events at the Centennial Exhibition just about to unfold, the young inventor had no idea of the celebrity, and the troubles, that were just around the corner for him. His train ride to Philadelphia would be a life-changing one.

Chapter 6
"Hoy! Hoy! Hoy!"

uoyed by his triumph at the Centennial, but worn out by all his other commitments, Alec needed a rest. He returned to Brantford later in the summer of 1876, taking the train from Boston through New York and Niagara Falls to Paris, Ontario. When he arrived in Paris in the wee hours of the morning, he was exhilarated by the Ontario summer night. It was comparatively cool after the suffocating heat of Philadelphia and Boston, and it felt so good to be home that he walked the rest of the way to the Bell homestead, some 16 kilometres away.

Cousins and an uncle from Australia had arrived for a family wedding and extended visit. It would be a time of relaxation and sociability. But, of course, for Alec, it was also a time for work. He had a plan to make the first long-distance call at home in Brantford.

In Boston, after the Centennial, Alec had tried to use the telephone along established telegraph wires for calls further away than 100 metres, but had not succeeded in transmitting a signal. This time, he was determined to make it work.

The first test he did took place on August 3. He set up his transmitter in Brantford and the receiver at the general store and telegraph office in Mount Pleasant, some eight kilometres away. This was a big event for the local townsfolk, who gathered in considerable numbers to see the invention young Alec Bell had come up with. He had arranged for his Uncle David to be at the transmitter, while he waited anxiously at the receiver. They had agreed on a crude communication system to overcome the limitations of a one-way phone; David would know that Alec was hearing him if he heard a break in the electrical current over the wire. They had also planned a "programme" of music and speech that David would perform.

At the appointed time, Alec picked up the receiver and heard ... nothing. He waited over 15 minutes for his uncle's voice to come over the wire. What had gone wrong? He finally realized that the operator had made a faulty connection, hastily corrected it, and with relief heard David lustily singing a song at the other end of the wire.

As the song finished, he sent the agreed-upon signal back to Brantford. David then launched into another tune before exclaiming, "Hoy! Hoy! Hoy!" For the public gathered in Mount Pleasant, David sang *God Save the Queen* and recited some of Shakespeare's work.

The evening was a hit with the people of Mount Pleasant, and Alec fell asleep that night full of pride and high hopes.

Energized by the excitement of the previous night, Alec planned to carry out his second test the very next day. He had decided that his telephone would be part of the evening's activities at the Bell homestead at Tutelo Heights. Melville and Eliza were holding a "champagne supper" in honour of his Australian uncle, Edward, and cousin Frances, who were soon to depart from Ontario and continue their North American travels.

Despite the sweltering heat, Alec spent the day stringing stovepipe wire from the house to the main telegraph line about 400 metres away. In order to reach this distance, he bought up all the iron wire in Brantford, and as he attached the wire to seemingly countless fence posts, he wondered if the effort would be worth it. But his enthusiasm for his new invention was boundless, so he worked away and tried to think cool thoughts.

That evening Alec set up his receiver on the porch at the house. The dinner guests on that warm summer night heard a series of songs transmitted through the air from one of the outbuildings back to the verandah. This was the first time Alec had tried to send three voices at once along the wire, and it worked just fine. This was important because it showed that "with the undulatory current a single transmitting instrument... will suffice for any number of simultaneous messages." He was elated, describing the experiment as "a perfect success."

The longest test yet was planned for August 10. Alec had written to the Dominion Telegraph Company, about 13 kilometres away in Paris, to see if he could use their lines for one hour to do a test that night. The story goes that the company manager in Paris tossed Alec's letter into the wastebasket, thinking that here was another crank who was surely playing with less than a full deck. The tests of the previous week had not received wide publicity, even locally, so it was not surprising that he had little faith in Alec's claims.

Fortunately, an office assistant retrieved the letter and thought it worthwhile to go over his boss's head. He contacted the Brantford manager and got permission from him to use the lines. However, all this red tape took some time to unravel, and Alec only received permission from the company at the last minute. He had to scramble to get everything ready.

With the entire plan looking uncertain, Melville had accepted another engagement for that evening in Hamilton. When word arrived that the test could go forward after all, he regretfully told his son that he would have to miss it in order to keep his other engagement. Alec was very disappointed that his father was not going to be able to be there to help him with this public test of the telephone. His father's approval was still very important to Alec. (He had been dismayed and angered only the year before when Melville had not immediately been in favour of Mabel Hubbard as Alec's future wife. Fortunately they resolved the issue, though Melville and Eliza had still not met their intended daughter-in-law.)

Once the trouble with the magnets was resolved, the evening was a resounding triumph. As in the first test, various songs were sung by the folk in Brantford and immediately recognized by those listening in Paris. And then Alec heard a voice he hadn't expected to hear — that of his father. Could the line have contorted his uncle's voice by some trick, making it sound like Melville's? Alec telegraphed to Brantford to ask if it really were his father, and Melville himself replied. He had cancelled his engagement and walked into Brantford to be a part of Alec's big moment. Alec's happiness with the evening, and with his three experiments, was complete.

Chapter 7
"Our Fortunes Are Made"

oon after this triumphant evening, Alec began to make his way back to Boston with his uncle and cousin. He yearned to be with Mabel again and to tell her in person everything he had accomplished over the weeks they had been apart. He was also most anxious to get back together with Watson and work on further improvements to the telephone. They needed to get two-way conversation going.

He knew he needed Watson's able hands to work on improving his telephone, so when he got back he offered his friend a deal too good to refuse: if Watson would come to work for Alec exclusively, he would earn $3 per day, free room and board, and a one-tenth interest in all of Alec's patents, including the telephone. Sanders and Hubbard were in favour of the plan. They were still paying Watson's salary, since Alec was as broke as ever. His successful experiments in Brantford notwithstanding, he was still some way from being able to make any money from his exciting new invention. Hubbard realized that Watson would help keep Alec on track, making sure he stayed with the project to fruition instead of racing off after some other new idea.

Watson and Alec worked away, making adjustments here and there, constantly testing the apparatus. They knew it was only a matter of time before the first two-way phone conversation happened. Hubbard threw his energies into promoting the telephone, since by now he had realized its great commercial potential.

Western Union was the obvious choice to get involved with the telephone in its embryonic state, since the vast company already had thousands of miles of telegraph wire laid and was in the best position to put the apparatus to use right away. But William Orton could not get over his enormous dislike of Gardiner Greene Hubbard. In the late fall of 1876, Orton made what was surely one of the worst business decisions ever, by refusing to buy the rights to the telephone for $100,000. While personal animosity may have come into the picture, a document from Western Union dated 1876 seems to show that someone, somewhere within the company, really underestimated the telephone at this time. The memo reads, in part, "This telephone has too many shortcomings to be considered as a means of communication. The device is inherently of no value to us."

On October 6 Alec and Watson were holed up in two different rooms of Alec's house, each with a transmitter/ receiver. The conversation that ensued was historic, if not particularly witty.

Alec began by saying, "If you understand what I say, say something to me."

Watson replied, "It is decidedly the best I ever heard."

Alec countered, "It is the best *I* ever heard."

The line was clear, as was every word spoken. Watson (perhaps realizing that posterity would want a more dignified repartee) noted, "Success has at last attended our efforts."

Alec, as usual, had the last word. "If only we can keep it always so, our fortunes are made," he mused gleefully.

Only a few days later, Alec and Watson tested their machines on a private telegraph line. With Alec in Boston and Watson in Cambridgeport, just over three kilometres distant, they had another conversation where each understood the other clearly. They talked back and forth for an hour and a half, doubtless discussing the immediate future of their wonderful invention.

By this time, Alec had been showing the telephone to academic audiences for several months. One memorable night, Alec presented his invention to the notoriously poker-faced members of the American Academy of Arts and Sciences. He allowed members of the audience to try the apparatus for themselves. To his delight, he received a round of applause from the Academy — the only lecturer ever to have been applauded. For all of us who now take the phone for granted, it's hard to imagine the amazement of these learned men on hearing one another's voices coming through the wire. They were absolutely flabbergasted. As Alec fell asleep that night, the applause of his fellow scientists still ringing in his ears, he thought, "This is the proudest and happiest night of my life."

He decided he should begin to hold public demonstrations, where curious members of the public would pay good money to see the telephone in action. By charging admission to his lectures, he could finally see some financial return from the machine, money that he could put aside for his eventual wedding day. The newspapers began to cover these demonstrations and Alec began to be better known.

Yet even with all the publicity and acceptance of his invention, Alec was already thinking new thoughts. He was canny enough to realize that the telephone was a wonderful invention, but he had dozens of other compelling ideas he wanted to explore. He was still a very young man, not yet 30 years old. He wanted to make money off the telephone, "to take off the hardships of life and leave me free to follow out the ideas that interest me most." He also needed money to get his foreign patents in order.

In January 1877, following his submission to the patent office of the far-reaching and thorough document that helped cement the invention as his own, Alec received a patent for further improvements to the telephone. It included using compound batteries in the telephone instead of magnets (an improvement suggested by Watson), which made for a much clearer transmission and reception.

In February, Alec presented the telephone to a sizable crowd in Salem, Massachusetts. Everyone in the crowd of 500 to 600 people (with the exception of his fiancée, who could only attempt to gauge the invention's reception by looking around at the faces in the audience) could hear the words transmitted. Watson was a full 30 kilometres away, singing and reciting into the receiver, delighting the crowd with his comments. The event went off well, despite a few hitches at the beginning of the presentation. Alec wrote to Hubbard, "As I placed my mouth to the instrument it seemed as if an electric thrill went through the audience — and that they recognized for the first time — what was meant by the 'Telephone.'" That evening, reporters submitted the first-ever newspaper report to be transmitted by telephone. It was published the next day in the *Boston Globe*.

With the publicity that was being generated, the inevitable naysayers began to emerge. The *Chicago Tribune* published an article a few days after the Salem demonstration, suggesting that Alec was a fraud. The *Tribune* claimed that not only had Alec *not* invented the telephone, but that he had, in fact, *stolen* the idea from Elisha Gray. (Gray had also hit the lecture circuit to promote his machine that transmitted musical tones.) When Alec confronted Gray about the article, he claimed innocence. The plans the two inventors had made after the Centennial Exhibition to work together had never come to pass, but at this point their relationship was still friendly, so Alec allowed his rival the benefit of the doubt. After all, Gray had a point; he couldn't control everything the newspapers chose to print.

Over the spring of 1877, Alec lectured and demonstrated the telephone to eager audiences. He did a repeat performance in Salem where he charged admission, clearing $149. Impulsively romantic, he spent over half of the money on a little model of a telephone in silver, as a gift for Mabel.

The first private telephone line was installed in Charles Williams's shop in Boston, connected to his home, which very probably made him the first man in history to be asked by his wife to pick up a loaf of bread on the way home from work.

Hubbard made the shrewd business decision to have the telephones available for lease, instead of for sale, which meant the original inventor and his partners could keep control of the business. Requests for machines began to pour in from forward-thinking members of the public. The units were manufactured in Williams's shop, stretching Thomas Sanders's dollars to the limit as the demand for telephones began to outstrip his wealth. In fact, Sanders nearly bankrupted himself in the early days to pay for the manufacture of all the telephones leased out by the company. He poured over $110,000 of his own money into the company to get the instrument launched. (While Hubbard was a wealthy man on paper, he had no liquidity, so his money was not easily acces-sible. His main contribution to the partnership was to market the telephone.)

By May 1877, anyone could rent a telephone for $20 per year for "social purposes connecting a dwelling house with any other building," or $40 per year for business purposes. The telephone, which consisted of a squat wooden box serv-ing as both transmitter and receiver, worked within distances of not more than 30 kilometres.

The partners realized that, as demand increased, they were going to have to become more organized in their endea-vour. In July 1877, just a few days before Alec and Mabel mar-ried, the Bell Telephone Company was born. Watson received his 10 percent, while each of the others received a third of what remained. All were to profit handsomely from the agreement. After the first rocky years of the Bell Telephone Company's existence, the investors were well rewarded for the risks they had taken on Alec's behalf when the company was reorganized and went public with very valuable shares.

Alec promptly gave all but 10 of his shares to Mabel as a wedding gift. He also gave her a cross made of pearls. They were married in a simple ceremony on July 11, 1877, at Mabel's home in Brattle Street, with the smell of lilies filling the warm evening air. Mabel was 19 and Alec 30, and both were immensely happy to be together.

They set out to honeymoon in Niagara Falls before trav-elling back to Brantford, where Mabel met her in-laws for the first time. A Scottish wedding tradition is to break an oatcake over the bride's head before she enters her new home with her husband. Generally this takes place at the wedding cere-mony, and it symbolizes the hope that the bride will never go hungry in her married life. Despite the continental European schooling of her younger days, Mabel was unaware of this tradition, and Alec hadn't thought to warn her.

As Alec and his young bride pulled up in front of the Bell homestead, the first thing Mabel saw was a small figure rushing out of the front door and down the steps. She pre-sumed this was Alec's mother, ready to greet her with a warm embrace. What Mabel didn't see was what the woman had in her hand — until WHACK! Eliza reached up and showered oaty crumbs all over Mabel's hair. Alec (and Melville, who had emerged from the house by now) roared with laughter while the new bride stood for a moment in stunned silence. A more surprising beginning to a relationship with one's in-laws would be hard to imagine. Who *were* these Scottish folk she was now related to? Fortunately, Mabel was able to take a joke, and once all was explained she began to feel more at home.

After a few weeks in Brantford, the happy couple made their way to Montreal and then to New York, to set sail on the SS *Anchoria* for Plymouth, England. Alec was to address the British Association for the Advancement of Science in Plymouth in the middle of August. As it turned out, they were to stay in Britain for over a year.

Chapter 8
"Everything Coming Out In Our Favour"

t was May 10, 1878. Alec and Mabel sat in their luxurious London home, looking in delight at their first daughter, who had been born two days earlier. The proud papa wrote home that night, "Such a funny little black thing it is! Perfectly formed — with a full crop of dark hair — bluish eyes — and a complexion so swarthy that Mabel declares she has given birth to a *red Indian!*" He also commented that, unlike either of her parents, she appeared to be very punctual, having arrived right on time. She went nameless for a few weeks until her parents settled on the moniker of Elsie May.

Due in part to Mabel's pregnancy and in part to Alec's business concerns, the Bells had been in England for almost a year when Elsie was born. They rented a 17-room house of some grandeur on Alec's reasoning that it was important to look as though they were prosperous, though at the time they engaged the house they had only a small income. Fortunately, a substantial sum of patent money came in at just the right time, signalling the beginning of financial security for the Bells.

Alec was a sensation when demonstrating the telephone to the British public. Everywhere he went he was invited to speak about it. However, due to mismanagement — and even outright fraud on the part of one manager — the telephone company he set up there not only failed to thrive, but almost shut down after a few years. Indeed, the patent money he was first paid, though equivalent to a year's salary, was only a fraction of what he should have received.

Alec preferred to have little to do with the daily affairs of the company, and it began to drift. Dismayed at this turn of events, his father-in-law eventually appeared on the scene to put the troubled British telephone company to rights, providing a substantial inheritance for his grandchildren in the process. Most of the money earned went into a trust fund, out of which Alec and Mabel received a generous yearly allowance. Since Alec freely admitted that he had no head for business, this was a wise course to follow.

While in Britain, Alec promoted the telephone constantly. William Thomson had addressed the British Association for the Advancement of Science back in August 1876, right after his return from the Centennial Exhibition. He had called

Alec's invention "the greatest by far of the all the marvels of the electric telegraph," and the most wonderful thing he had seen in America. (It was later to win the Centennial Medal, for which Thomson had been one of the judges.)

British audiences proved to be just as eager as the Americans to hear this marvellous new invention for themselves. Alec found himself at the centre of a great deal of attention, and Mabel went right along with it. Despite her deafness, she was a sparkling asset to Alec at dinner parties and social gatherings and was able to follow conversation just fine, as long as the speaker looked right at her.

A royal invitation arrived in December. Alec was invited to demonstrate the telephone to Queen Victoria at Osborne House, her private retreat on the Isle of Wight. Mabel was thrilled. Naturally, her first thought was, "What shall I wear?" She began a search for the perfect gown. She found one in Paris — where else? Now she was all set to meet the most powerful woman in the world, and to see her royal residence.

As Alec and the Queen's secretary, Sir Thomas Biddulph, wrote back and forth to arrange the date, it became clear to Biddulph that the inventor was planning on bringing his wife along. He wrote and gently broke the news that Mabel was not invited. "I do not see how I can manage for Mrs. Bell to come here on Monday. I should hardly like to ask the Queen, and could not propose it otherwise."

So Mabel lost her chance to meet the Queen. Presumably, she kept the dress.

Alexander Graham Bell

Alec arranged for a musical performance for Her Majesty, which would come over the telephone from various other cities in Britain. These calls — linking Cowes, Southampton, and London with the Queen — are considered the first public long-distance calls in the United Kingdom. He also ran a line from Osborne House to Thomas Biddulph's cottage on the grounds so the Queen could speak to her secretary by telephone. The members of the royal family then amused themselves by talking to each other on the telephone, with exceptional clarity. The royal family had such fun that the demonstration went on for almost three hours.

Alec received a letter a few days later from Biddulph, asking if the Queen could purchase the telephones that had been left there after the demonstration. He replied with an offer to custom-make some telephones "expressly for her Majesty's use," and created some more royal-looking phones with ivory handsets.

When Alec later described Victoria to his wife in private, he used the words "humpy, stumpy, dumpy." He also commented on her red face and hands, which brought to his mind those of a washerwoman. However, he was very pleased and honoured by her reception of his invention.

Alec made one appalling faux pas during his visit to the Queen. He had arranged for a woman to sing a particular tune over the telephone. At the moment the song was about to begin, the monarch was looking away and not paying attention to the device. To get Her Majesty's attention, Alec did what came naturally to him: he touched her hand, as he would have with any one of his deaf students. He had forgotten that court protocol dictated nobody touched the Queen! Fortunately, she was so captivated with the rest of the presentation that she made no fuss about the event, though it gave the courtiers something to talk about.

Victoria's warm reception of the telephone doubtless helped fuel its popularity in Britain. It was doing well in the United States as well. The trust fund that Hubbard had set up would allow not only for Alec's children to benefit from his invention, but for him and Mabel to receive a healthy income as well. It looked as if the fame and fortune that Alec had dreamed of was finally to be his.

And then Western Union tried to take it all away.

Despite William Orton's assertion in 1876 that the telephone would never become commercially valuable, Western Union went into the telephone business very quickly after Bell telephones began to be available for lease. Operating as the American Speaking Telephone Company, and capitalizing on its huge network of existing telegraph lines, Western Union took little time to become a serious threat. The company infringed blatantly on Alec's patent, and, to add insult to injury, Western Union now proclaimed that Alec was not the true inventor of the telephone, but had stolen the idea from Elisha Gray.

As the months dragged on and Western Union's advertising continued to malign Alec, he grew fed up with the whole thing. "Why should it matter to the world who invented the telephone, so long as the world gets the benefit of it?" he railed.

Sometimes he seemed to think, naively, that having the truth on his side would be enough to vindicate his name. Other times he felt it wasn't important whether or not he got his due credit, as long as he made enough money from the invention and his family believed in him.

The one thing he didn't want to do, angry though he was, was fight. He had many ideas in his head for what he wanted to do with the rest of his life — being tied up in court battles was not one of them. He begged Mabel, "Let me go back to the work I love [teaching the deaf] if I can find support for us both." He made plans to establish a school for the deaf in Greenock, Scotland, and actually went away to Greenock to teach for a short period of time, leaving Mabel with baby Elsie in London.

He was invited to give some lectures at Oxford on the subject of speech and decided to return to Canada shortly afterwards to start a new life there with his family. Alec was so annoyed with the bureaucracy surrounding the telephone — the lawsuits and filing for patents — that in September 1878 he declared dramatically, "Of one thing I am quite determined and that is to waste no more time and money upon the Telephone ... I am sick of the Telephone and have done with it for altogether."

It seemed as if he was just going to let all his hard-earned success slip away from him.

Here again, Gardiner Greene Hubbard came to the rescue. Hubbard realized that Western Union was going to run Bell Telephone out of business if they didn't fight back against the giant company. Thomas Sanders now provided funds to hire some very smart lawyers and go to court. While Alec and Mabel were still in England, a lengthy legal battle began as Bell Telephone sued the American Speaking Telephone Company (Western Union) for patent infringement.

Mabel's father wrote Alec increasingly desperate letters with news of the lawsuit, trying to engage Alec's interest. Hubbard had to make his stubborn son-in-law see that if he did not take the matter seriously and testify on his own behalf in the lawsuit, he might lose everything. He even wrote to Alec's father, Melville, imploring him to make sure Alec realized how serious things were. Since Alec and Mabel were travelling to Brantford to see his parents, Hubbard thought that perhaps Melville could talk some sense into his son.

Mabel and Alec returned from England to Canada in November, and an agitated Tom Watson was there to meet them when the ship landed in Quebec. He had been despatched by Gardiner Greene Hubbard to get Alec back to Boston at all costs and as soon as possible, before their time in court was up and the case turned over to the other side for their testimony. Grumbling, but finally acquiescent, Alec agreed to go back and appear in court, provided the Bell Telephone Company would pay his expenses. First, he insisted on taking Mabel and Elsie to Brantford. Watson accompanied them in order to keep a close eye on Alec and make sure he actually returned to Boston.

When Alec finally arrived in Boston and took the stand, he proved to be a magnificent witness. He had excellent recall of the chain of events that led to the invention of the telephone. He understood the science behind his idea and was able to put it across in the courtroom. And, of course, as usual, his elocution and demeanour were utterly dignified and convincing.

After more than a year of legal wrangling, Western Union was unable to disprove the fact that Alec had really invented the telephone. Elisha Gray had filed a caveat — a statement that he *intended to work on* a device to transmit speech — a few hours after Alec had applied for a patent on a machine that *actually could transmit* speech. Back when Gray and Alec were still corresponding in a friendly way, Gray himself had written to Alec, "I do not, however, claim even the credit of inventing it, as I do not believe a mere description of an idea that has never been *reduced* to *practice*, — in the *strict sense* of that phrase, — should be dignified with the name invention."

While Gray gamely testified in the case, it was this admission, as much as anything, that sank Western Union's case. Reportedly, Gray glumly told his attorney, "I must swear *to* it. You can swear *at* it!"

Alec, hearing of Gray's testimony, wrote to Mabel, "Poor

Mr. Gray. I feel sorry for him — for I feel sure he would never of his own accord have allowed himself to be placed in the painful position in which he now is — that is upon the supposition that he is an honourable man." This was a supposition that Alec, generously, always made of people he encountered until proven otherwise.

The Bell Telephone Company victory was detailed in the *Boston Daily Advertiser*.

SATURDAY MORNING, OCT. 25, 1879.
THE TELEPHONE SETTLEMENT.
The rival and conflicting interests in the various telephone patents have at last been harmonized, and Professor Bell is master of the field ... The Western Union Telegraph Company ... agrees to withdraw from the telephone business in the United States, leaving the field entirely clear to the company operating under the Bell patents. All persons who hold rights from other companies will be licensed under these patents. The Western Union further agrees to allow the Bell Telephone Company a percentage on the telegraphic business received through its instruments, and to co-operate to the extent of its power.

Under this adjustment the Bell Telephone Company acquires all the telephonic inventions of Elisha Gray of Chicago, of Thomas A. Edison, of

George M. Phelps, and all others who had assigned their interests to the Western Union or other allied companies. The right to connect telephonic district or exchange systems remains exclusively with the Bell Company, which will also license the Western Union to use the telephone for transmitting telegraphic messages. The compromise thus not only secures freedom from litigation and control of all the patents now out for the purpose of transmitting human speech, but establishes harmony of interests between the Western Union and the new company, which must be of inestimable value to both ...

Now that litigation is ended and the world is all before it, the Bell telephone has a future of fame and fortune in store for it not surpassed by any of the great discoveries of our time.

In exchange for this major victory, Bell Telephone had to pay Western Union 20 percent of its profits from the telephone for the next 17 years. (Since Western Union's inventors had come up with some good improvements and innovations to Alec's original apparatus, this must have seemed a reasonable compromise to all involved.)

Despite the fact that Alec had won a decisive legal victory against one of America's biggest companies, other competitors began to emerge from the woodwork, coming forth time and again to try their luck against Bell Telephone. Often it was dishonest individuals or companies hoping to make a quick buck from his invention until they were taken to court, although once in a while a person came along who really seemed to believe that he had invented the telephone. The Bell Telephone Company took on challengers over 600 times in the next 18 years, when the original patent ran out.

They never once lost a case.

Chapter 9
"I Have Really Accomplished a Great Work"

he first court victory meant Alec and Mabel's financial future was now assured. They were a wealthy young couple, and Alec could afford to dabble in whatever profession he chose. They decided to move to Washington, DC, to be closer to the Hubbards. In time the elder Bells moved down from Brantford to be nearer to the rest of the family.

Alec kept on inventing, following, as he had dreamed, the things that interested him most. Tellingly, he wrote to Mabel in 1879, "I can't bear to hear that even my friends should think that I stumbled upon an invention and that there is no more good in me." He spent the rest of his life working on countless projects, often with a humanitarian

aim. It would be over two decades before his next great calling appeared. In the meantime, he travelled and enjoyed life
with his beloved wife and family, while constantly thinking of
new ideas to improve the world.

Alec and Mabel had a second daughter, Marian, in
February 1880. At the time, Alec was working on a precursor
to the cordless phone, which allowed sound to travel along
rays of light. He called this device a photophone. The week
Marian (who was always called Daisy) was born, he was
making progress with his experiments and was jubilant at
his new invention. Mabel joked to her family that he had to
be dissuaded from calling his new daughter "Photophone."
Alec never went much further with his research on the photophone — he was well ahead of his time on this invention
that, over a hundred years later, would become a reality with
the invention of fibre optics.

In later years Mabel bore two premature sons, Edward
in 1881 and Robert in 1883. Sadly, neither lived longer than a
few hours due to problems with their underdeveloped lungs.
Alec felt they could have survived if they had been given
some help with breathing, for they were healthy in other
respects. He set to work on inventing a "vacuum jacket" that
would act as a bellows to help such children breathe. (He later
tested this invention on a sheep in Nova Scotia, which he had
drowned for the purpose. He managed to bring it back to life,
to the bemusement and fear of his superstitious employees
there.) Alec's vacuum jacket concept laid the foundations for

the invention of the iron lung, which was later to save the lives of thousands of children afflicted by polio.

Alec constantly sought ways to assist people through his inventions. When an unhappy political candidate shot American president James Garfield in early July of 1881, Alec felt that he had an invention that could help.

The bullet was lodged somewhere in the president's body. If it could be found, his doctors could extract it and he might live; if not, he would surely die a long, slow death. Many doctors went to Washington to see if they could find the bullet, sticking various fingers and instruments into the bullet hole. This was before the concepts of sterilization and cleanliness had entered the medical field.

Alec's invention was an electrical probe, which he called an "induction balance," that vibrated when it came into contact with metal. He had tested it out at home in his lab, and on veterans with shrapnel still inside their bodies, and had found it to work very well.

Alec went to the executive mansion and rigged up his wires in the sickroom where the president was confined. Garfield had been shot several weeks previously, and was in great pain by that time. Alec wrote to Mabel, "His face is very pale — or rather it is of an ashen grey colour which makes one feel for a moment that you are not looking upon a living man ... It made my heart bleed to look at him and think of all he must have suffered to bring him to this."

Alec ran the induction balance over the president's

body in the area where Garfield's doctors thought the bullet must be. There was no reaction from the probe. He tried again, but still nothing happened. He was mystified. The probe had worked fine before this. Had the doctors removed all the metal from near the president's body, as he had specified? Perhaps it was the coils on the mattress that ruined the reception. In any case, he never managed to find the bullet that nestled insidiously inside Garfield's body, despite repeated efforts.

Garfield died several weeks later, not so much from his bullet wound as from infection and bungled surgeries to remove the bullet. Possibly he would have lived if all the medical experts of the day had simply left him alone.

After the post-mortem on the president, Alec found out that the bullet had not been in any area of Garfield's body that he had explored with the induction balance. He was devastated that his instrument had failed and might now be seen with scorn by the medical profession and the world at large. "I feel all the more mortified — because I feel that I have really accomplished a great work — and have devised an apparatus that will be of inestimable use in surgery." He was right. The successor to the induction balance, which he called a telephone probe, saved countless lives during several wars, locating bullets and shrapnel in wounded soldiers in the days before the X-ray began to be used. (Incidentally, Alec was reportedly the first man to take an X-ray when this new device appeared in Canada.) In recognition of this valuable invention, Alec was granted an honourary M.D. from the University of Heidelberg.

In 1880 Alec began receiving letters from the French consul. Assuming they were related to his telephone patent in France, he didn't even open them, simply passing them on to Hubbard to be dealt with. Finally, someone in England mailed him a congratulatory letter and a newspaper clipping, telling him that the Académie française had awarded him the Volta Prize. He had been recognized as "the inventor of the best application of electricity."

He travelled to Paris to receive the prize, which he felt confirmed once and for all that he was the inventor of the telephone. It meant a great deal to him in terms of professional recognition.

Of course, the money (50,000 francs, or $10,000 in the dollars of the day) was a welcome windfall, which he decided to put towards his laboratory and library. With two other partners, he set up the "Volta Associates" to do further research into electrical matters, and the three men began to tinker with an invention called the phonograph in 1881.

Thomas Edison, the inventor of the electric light bulb, had patented the phonograph three years earlier. It involved a tinfoil cylinder with an attached stylus that recorded sound waves into the tinfoil. The world's first recording was Edison, reciting "Mary Had a Little Lamb." Edison felt his machine might have some practical business applications (as an early type of Dictaphone machine) but then began to investigate

Alexander Graham Bell opening the New York–
Chicago long-distance line, October 18, 1898

other ideas that took him in a different direction. He didn't
follow up on improving the phonograph.

One of the major drawbacks of Edison's tinfoil cylinder
was the impermanence of the markings made by the stylus.
The sound waves could be preserved better in some other
medium, reasoned the Volta Associates, and they tried many

a medium before discovering that recordings made on wax were permanent. This improvement suddenly made the phonograph much more useful. The other major improvement that came of the associates' tinkering was a floating stylus.

The three partners received a patent (generally referred to as the Tainter patent, after the Volta partner who suggested the idea of the floating stylus) for these improvements in May 1886. They called their machine a "graphophone." The first recording the trio made was rather quirky: "There are more things in heaven and earth, Horatio, than are dreamed of in our philosophy ... I am a Graphophone and my mother was a Phonograph."

Both the Tainter and Edison phonograph patents were eventually sold to Jesse Lippincott, a wealthy businessman who used the technology to form the North American Phonograph Company. While this company went bankrupt only two years later, the sale of the patent rights made the fortunes of the Volta Associates. Alec, who was already wealthy from his shares in Bell Telephone, used his $200,000 to establish the Volta Bureau, which had as its goal "the increase and diffusion of knowledge relating to the Deaf." This bureau is still in existence today, though it is now called the Alexander Graham Bell Association for the Deaf and Hard of Hearing.

* * *

"I Have Really Accomplished a Great Work"

One final event of note during these years had a tremendous impact on the lives of the Bell family: their personal discovery of the village of Baddeck, on Cape Breton Island, Nova Scotia.

For many years Alec had suffered from the soggy summer heat of Boston and Washington. Summers caused him discomfort, and could be quite painful when the heat caused one of his lengthy headaches. He yearned for the cool and misty Scottish weather of his youth. Mabel wanted to find a place where the girls could wear trousers and the whole family could enjoy a casual lifestyle. For several summers they tried various seaside and lakeside resorts, but nothing seemed to fit.

In the summer of 1885 the family, along with Alec's father, Melville, set out on a holiday to Newfoundland. Melville had spent time there as a youth and had always credited the clean air there with restoring his vitality. Perhaps, thought Alec, Newfoundland will be the place where we can find our true home.

On the way, they took a detour to visit one of Gardiner Greene Hubbard's business interests, the Caledonia coal mine at Glace Bay on Cape Breton. Then the family boarded a boat that travelled on the large saltwater lake known as Bras d'Or Lake. One of the stops was Baddeck. Alec had recently read a book called "Baddeck, and That Sort of Thing," by a travel writer named Charles Dudley Warner. He therefore wanted to stop in at this charming small town to see it for himself.

When they arrived in Baddeck, the Bells were enchanted. The landscape, and the residents with their "Mc" and "Mac" surnames, reminded Alec of Scotland. It was entirely refreshing and beautiful.

It felt like home.

Before they left, they bought a farmhouse, and had decided to purchase land on the peninsula known as Red Head in order to build an estate there. This was to be their summer home for the next 37 years.

It took several years to buy the land they wanted — it had been subdivided into a dozen parcels with different owners — but when it was theirs, they named the estate Beinn Bhreagh (pronounced "Ben Vree-ah"), which is Gaelic for "Beautiful Mountain." The first dwelling they built was an enormous cottage with soaring wood timbers, known as "The Lodge." After a few years they built a much larger stone house high on the red cliffs above Baddeck Bay, which they named Beinn Bhreagh Hall. Completed in 1893 for $21,000, this imposing mansion has a perfect view from every window. It still belongs to the Bell descendants today.

Beinn Bhreagh became Alec and Mabel's family home, where they raised their daughters and, eventually, where their grandchildren would spend many enchanted summers. In the early days, they churned their own butter for fun. (It turned out to be not so much fun, so Alec rigged up a windmill to do the work.) Alec floated in the lake for hours, smoking a cigar and looking up at the night sky. Mabel became

Alexander Graham Bell and family, ca. 1909, Baddeck, Nova Scotia

very involved in the life of the village and founded the Young Ladies' Club of Baddeck to "stimulate the acquisition of general knowledge" among the Baddeck women.

Visitors were always welcome — sometimes Alec, absent-mindedly, would even invite scientists who were famously opposed to each other in their beliefs, which made for excitable debates.

Baddeck became a new "dreaming place" for Alec and opened a whole new chapter in his inventing life. At a time when many people begin to think about retirement, he was about to launch himself into the skies with some of his most innovative work yet.

Chapter 10
"It Will All Be UP With Us Someday!"

n the last years of the 19th century, Alec turned his fertile brain to a puzzle that had intrigued him from the time he was a boy in Scotland: flight. Ever since he could remember, birds had fascinated him, and he spent hours dreaming of flight while watching their graceful movements. Like many dreamers before him, he felt that figuring out how the birds flew would unlock the secret of flight, making it possible for people, too, to take to the skies.

Conventional wisdom at the time held that flying machines were impossible. Even the most eminent scientists of the day mocked the idea of men being able to fly. William Thomson (by this time Lord Kelvin), who had been so enthusiastic about the telephone, expressed his disappointment that

Alec was now pursuing aeronautics. In 1896, Kelvin had these derisive words to say about flight: "I have not the smallest molecule of faith in aerial navigation other than ballooning ... I would not care to be a member of the Aeronautical Society."

Alec was too fired up with the idea of flight to pay much attention to his detractors. He had made a friend who believed as much as he did: Samuel Pierpont Langley. When Alec first heard of Langley's work in aviation, he travelled from Baddeck to Washington expressly to meet him, braving the summer heat which he described as "Awful — frightful — h-ll-sh!"

He wrote to Mabel shortly afterwards. "Langley's flying machines — They flew for me today. I shall have to make experiments upon my own account in Cape Breton. Can't keep out of it. It will be all *UP* with us someday!"

Shared enthusiasm gave the two inventors an immediate bond, and Langley and Alec became fast friends. From then on they kept up a lively correspondence related to flight, trading ideas and information on their various experiments. Alec even contributed $5000 of his own money to help Langley with his work.

Langley was no amateur crank, but a respected scientist and the secretary of the Smithsonian Institution. He was a largely self-taught genius, with interests ranging widely from math to astronomy to physics. Despite his intelligence and his very public position, he was a very shy person, fearful of ridicule if his theories failed. As the only leading American scientist of the day who openly proclaimed a belief in the possibility of flight, he came in for his share of teasing in the press. Mabel wrote of Langley, "Of course the papers treat him more respectfully than they would anyone else, still they cannot resist a sly joke now and again."

As early as 1893, Alec, too, was boldly asserting that there would be flight within 10 years. The key was to figure out how to include an engine that was strong enough to power the plane, but light enough to be lifted off the ground. "The more I experiment, the more convinced I become that flying machines are practical."

Alec was soon to be proved right. In the very same year that Lord Kelvin flippantly dismissed aerial navigation (1896), Alec and Langley actually witnessed one of Langley's model airplanes in flight.

Langley had contacted Alec to let him know that he was ready to test out one of his "aerodromes." His cabled invitation was a masterpiece of underselling. "I expect to take the 4.25 P.M. train ... to-morrow for Quantico, and to spend the night there, hoping to make the trial in the morning. I am bound to say in advance that the prospects are not good for success, but if you will take the chance of a fruitless journey, I shall be delighted to have you come. May I expect to meet you at the station?"

Alec, of course, couldn't resist the chance to see a machine in flight, and arrived shortly afterwards at Langley's houseboat on the Potomac River, where his friend had set up a launching pad for his steam-powered machine. Very early in the morning, the two inventors were out on the deck, giddy with excitement. Langley prepared his 'drome — a steam-powered biplane driven by a propeller — and both men watched intently as the machine was catapulted into the air.

To their amazed delight, the aerodrome flew on its own.

It remained in the air for about 800 metres, reaching a height of about 30 metres. Alec later described its flight as that of a large bird, "sweeping steadily upward in a spiral path." Wisely, Alec grabbed his camera to capture an image of the machine soaring above the water. Langley would need visual proof to convince the public of his achievement.

When it ran out of steam, the 'drome landed gracefully in the water "and was immediately picked out and ready to be tried again." Langley's experiment was an unqualified success. The men flew the machine again with a similar result, and both knew that aviation history had been made. As Alec said, "No one could have witnessed these experiments without being convinced that the practicability of mechanical flight had been demonstrated."

Later that night, still buzzing from the excitement of the day, Alec wrote to his friend, thanking him for the opportunity to be present for such a momentous event. He was so overwhelmed that he put the wrong year on his letter — 1895 instead of 1896.

"I can't go to bed to-night without writing to thank you

for the confidence you have shown in me, by permitting me to witness your experiments today. Although, as you know, my mind was (theoretically at least) quite prepared for the result, I must confess that it was rather a startling experience actually to see a steam-engine flying in the air like a bird. I only hope that your success has been half as gratifying to you as it has been to me. I shall count this day as one of the most memorable of my life."

After this momentous occasion, Alec returned to Baddeck to continue his experiments with kites, seeking always to engineer safety and stability into his contraptions. He knew that flight could be dangerous — a European aviation pioneer died in 1896 while experimenting with flying — so Alec was determined to be safety-conscious above all.

He began his work in earnest in the last few years of the 19th century, about the same time that two other aviation pioneers, Orville and Wilbur Wright, were also exploring flight with kites. These magnificent kites bore little resemblance to a traditional children's toy. The Wrights' kites were biplane in nature, while at first Alec used a variety of kites to learn more about the air currents around Baddeck. One local resident remembered looking up at night into the sky over Baddeck Bay to see "dozens of large coloured paper balloons, fashioned in many shapes such as giant men, horses, cows, elephants, etc., and lighted and glowing," all sent up by the inventor at Beinn Bhreagh.

Alec spent several summers at Baddeck with his kites,

often missing out on various travels with his family to keep on working. He tried many shapes and forms: a three-wheeled kite, huge rings, and various blocky-looking kites. He was determined to launch a man-carrying kite, but not until he had unlocked the secret of keeping stability along with achieving lift.

During the course of his research, he came up with the idea of the tetrahedron. He ended up patenting this concept of a triangular pyramid, which offers exceptional three-dimensional strength while being very lightweight. Tetrahedral cells became the basic building blocks of his kites and many other structures that he built.

Over time, a large workshop was set up at Beinn Bhreagh to build kites. Alec employed many townspeople there. Local women sewed the silk tetrahedral cells while local men helped assemble and launch the kites, photograph them in the air, and record the experiment results.

On windy days a kite was always sure to be going up. Alec used red silk for the cells, so that every kite stood out sharply against the sky — key for obtaining good photographs, of course, but also simply beautiful and exhilarating to see. The inventor worked alongside his employees, running through the grass at the kite launch site, enjoying the hard work and pure pleasure of discovery.

Things were not going so happily for Samuel Langley. For some years he worked on a new aerodrome, this time a full-scale flying machine that could carry a pilot. While building the craft, he was forced to work under sustained media scrutiny. Based on the documented achievement of his earlier aerodromes, the US government had put $50,000 towards developing the machine, and the newspapers were enthusiastically covering the development of what they felt sure would be a boondoggle.

To Langley's anguish, at its official launch in December 1903, "Langley's Folly" crashed straight into the Potomac after its wing tore in half. The pilot had a close call, but fortunately was not killed.

Langley had contributed $20,000 of his own money to the project, so its failure was a considerable financial blow to him. However, it was the scorn and ridicule he was subjected to that really hurt. In the papers, it was said that "the only thing he ever made fly was Government money." At best, people thought he was a dreaming fool, at worst a charlatan. He was heartbroken, and retired from aerial experimentation after this failure.

Alec sympathized with his friend, and staunchly defended him by saying that "the apparatus caught in the launching ways, and was precipitated into the water without having a chance to show what it could do in the air ... there was no more reason for declaring it a failure than for deciding that a ship would not float that has never been launched." When Langley died only a few years later, Alec blamed the newspapers. "There can be little doubt that the unjust treatment to which he was exposed contributed materially to the production of the illness that caused his death."

A mere nine days after Langley's machine had its spectacular crash, the Wright brothers flew for the first time, in a private experimental attempt, at Kitty Hawk, North Carolina.

Chapter 11
"To Get a Man Into the Air"

lec was so excited by the astonishing feat of the two bicycle mechanics from Ohio that he became even more determined to launch a flying machine himself. He kept working on his kites, and he followed the continuing exploits of the Wrights closely for several years.

Even though the Wright brothers were highly secretive and would not fly in public, they published reports about their aeronautical firsts, and applied for patents on their flying machines. Many people doubted they had actually flown, since there was no visual proof, but Alec needed no convincing. Soon he found several other men who believed it was possible too.

In 1907, the Aerial Experiment Association was formed

in Baddeck, Nova Scotia, with Alexander Graham Bell as its chairman and driving force. It had a simple but dramatic goal: "To get a man into the air."

It was a small group, five members only, all of them talented men with an interest in flight. The four other men were all a good deal younger than Alec, but their youth was an asset, since Alec was already 60 years old by this time. As always, he had plenty of ideas and, as always, he needed someone else behind him to keep him on track.

They didn't have much time: all the members agreed that the association had to achieve its goals within one year. Each member would see one of his designs built and launched by the group. If, at the end of the year, it looked like they were getting somewhere and needed more time, they could extend the term. The short time frame must have sharpened everyone's wits, for they produced an impressive fleet over a period of only a few months.

The AEA was Mabel's idea, and it was funded almost entirely by her as well. She spent $35,000 of her own money to finance the research of the group, in which she believed passionately. Alec was happy to work with his wife on this important project, and felt himself revitalized by discussing ideas and plans with his four young men: Douglas McCurdy, F.W. "Casey" Baldwin, Glenn Curtiss, and Lt. Thomas Selfridge.

Alec and Mabel had known J.A.D. (Douglas) McCurdy since he was a very young boy. A Baddeck native, he was the son of one of their best friends there. In fact, when Arthur

Alexander Graham Bell

Dr. and Mrs. Alexander Graham Bell in their
motorboat *Ranzo* at Beinn Bhreagh, August 20, 1914

McCurdy's wife died, Alec and Mabel offered to adopt young
Douglas. Their offer was not taken up, but throughout his
boyhood Douglas was frequently to be found at Beinn
Bhreagh, helping Alec with his kite experiments. His interest
in this work led him to study engineering at the University
of Toronto.

"To Get a Man Into the Air"

In 1906, Mabel wrote to McCurdy as he was about to graduate from U of T and asked him to come back to Baddeck to work with Alec, and to bring a friend with him to help with tetrahedral and aviation research. McCurdy looked no further than young Casey Baldwin, who jumped at the chance to work with the famous inventor in his exciting new field.

Alec met Glenn Curtiss in 1906 at an aeronautical show where Alec was displaying his kites, while Curtiss was demonstrating his engines. Curtiss owned his own firm in Hammondsport, New York, where he built motorcycle engines. Alec ordered an engine from Curtiss for use in one of the big kites. The young engine expert then turned up at Beinn Bhreagh with an even more powerful engine, got interested in the experiments, and decided to stay for a while.

Lt. Thomas Selfridge, a young American army officer with a keen interest in the possible military applications of flight, became involved with the group after contacting Alec to ask about his kite experiments in 1907. Alec's response was typical: "Come on out to Baddeck and see what we are up to." In the fall of that year, Alec contacted President Roosevelt to ask for Selfridge to be detailed to Baddeck in an official capacity. The president granted his request, as long as Selfridge shared information about the goings-on at Baddeck with the US Army.

Once the group was formally established, they agreed to design and build five machines. They would work together on all the machines, with each member taking a turn at signing off on a final design. They spent their days designing and building. Their evenings were filled with lively discussions about any matter under the sun that interested the assorted company gathered at Beinn Bhreagh. Sometimes Alec would play piano and there would be a rousing singsong. With Elsie and Daisy grown and gone by this time, Alec and Mabel loved their group of young men as if they were a second family. Mabel was delighted when Casey Baldwin called her "the little mother of us all."

The first task the AEA took on was the launch of a massive kite, a tetrahedral monster that was Alec's brainchild. (Despite the Wrights' proven track record with biplanes, Alec was still firmly fixed on kites as the air vehicles of the future.) He had been working on the kite for some time already, with the help of his first two young helpers, McCurdy and Baldwin. On December 6, 1907, the *Cygnet* was finally launched.

It was a beautiful early winter day on the Bras d'Or Lakes. A steamer towed a second boat, which was carrying the *Cygnet* over Baddeck Bay. This man-carrying kite had a wingspan of 13.12 metres and was 3.36 metres tall. The idea was to test the kite under tow before trying to install a light engine and letting it soar free on future flights.

Lt. Thomas Selfridge was selected to take part in the first flight. He lay down like a larva inside a cocoon at the centre of the kite, from which he could see nothing of the landscape below him. Surrounded by almost 3400 cells of red silk, he was about to have the ride of his life.

The steamer began to gather speed, lifting the kite gently into the sky. It stayed aloft for about seven minutes and reached a height of about 50 metres, while going about 50 kilometres per hour. As it began to come down, however, Selfridge was blinded by the smoke from the steamer's stack, and didn't realize he should cut the tow-rope until he felt the icy blast of the Little Bras d'Or Lake take his breath away. He realized he had already hit the water!

The onlookers were alarmed as they watched the kite getting dragged further into the lake. The experiment was going horribly wrong.

But Selfridge finally emerged on shore, having disentangled himself from the silk and swum to safety. He was towelled off, wrapped in blankets, and given a stiff shot of whisky. Once he was safe, the kite experiment was deemed a success. They had proven beyond a doubt that, under the right conditions, the tetrahedral construction would be stable and safe for a man to fly.

However, the plan to put an engine into a kite had to be put on hold indefinitely, since *Cygnet* had sunk to the bottom of Baddeck Bay, where it rests to this day. Alec wanted to continue pursuing kite construction, but the rest of the group had another plan: to construct and launch a biplane.

Selfridge was the next to have a go at designing an aerodrome. (Alec continued to call airplanes "aerodromes" out of respect for Samuel Langley, who had coined the term. He felt it was more precise.) The young lieutenant contacted the

Wright brothers, who sent him some of their own research, designs, and information. After only a few months of work, a machine was completed. It was known as *Red Wing*, for its wings covered in red silk.

Red Wing was created in Hammondsport, New York, on the shores of Keuka Lake where Glenn Curtiss's engine manufacturing company was located, after the group decided to move their operations there for the winter.

On March 12, 1908, Casey Baldwin was the first to pilot *Red Wing*, since Selfridge had to miss the launch of his design due to a serious illness. The fragile little plane glided along the ice of Keuka Lake for about 100 metres, then rose about 3 metres into the air and flew for nearly another 100 metres.

This unprecedented event was noted in the local press as "the first successful public flight of a heavier than air flying machine in America." (By this time, the Wright brothers had been flying for some time, but their flights were always shrouded in secrecy.)

The newspaper report, while accurate, fails to convey the excitement the members of the AEA must have felt when they saw their "little red baby" fly for the first time. Only a few months before, none of them had even seen an airplane — and now one of their designs had actually taken wing before a crowd of people. It was a day none of them would ever forget.

As Alec noted in his journal that night, "Our only regret is that Lieut. Selfridge was not here to witness the success of the experiment."

Only a few days later, though, *Red Wing* was totalled in a crash on a snowy, rainy, windy day. The little plane suffered from a serious lack of lateral control and stability, which meant it could not fly straight when buffeted by wind. The precipitation added to the weight of the plane by soaking the fabric covering the wings. It was back to the drawing board, and this time it was Casey Baldwin overseeing the work. At least the engine was saved, and it went into the next couple of designs. The AEA applied their combined problem-solving skills to meet the lateral stability challenge.

Only a few months later, a second plane, *White Wing*, took to the skies. (They had run out of red silk and had used white muslin to cover the wings instead.) Baldwin flew it first, and then Thomas Selfridge took the controls. Alec noted, "The second flight was an inspiring spectacle. The White Wing left the ground and soared as gracefully as a bird for more than 240 feet [75 metres] at an elevation of 20 feet [six metres]. There was no apparent reason except the inexperience of the operator to prevent the continuation of the flight indefinitely." Indeed, Glenn Curtiss flew it over 300 metres a few days later.

White Wing featured two important innovations that are still used on airplanes today: ailerons, or wing flaps, to help achieve stability in the air, and landing gear (theirs was a three-wheeled affair).

Unfortunately, *White Wing* came to the same end as its predecessor, crashing a few days after its launch and ending up in pieces. The men got back to work, this time on a Glenn Curtiss design that Alec dubbed *June Bug*. To add a bit of spice to the goings-on, the magazine *Scientific American* had offered a prize for the first flying machine to cover a distance of more than one kilometre. The magazine's editor had expected the Wright brothers to rise to the challenge, but they were still working in secrecy and didn't rise to the bait. The AEA, whose members were far from shy of publicity, set their sights on the prize.

June Bug took to the sky in late June of 1908. The group members got in touch with the Aero Club of America to announce that they were ready to try for the *Scientific American* Cup. The exciting event was set to be part of the July 4th celebrations at Hammondsport, where there were sure to be plenty of spectators to heighten the excitement.

The day of the flight was cool and rainy, with winds that made flying unlikely, but by evening the winds had died down and the crowd was eager to see what *June Bug* could do. Curtiss took the 'drome up, but it flew much higher than he had intended, about 12 metres in the air. He felt uncomfortable going so high. He decided to bring the plane back down and figure out what was happening. After a few adjustments he took off again, this time flying about a kilometre and a half, well past the necessary one kilometre mark. He made a graceful landing to capture the prize on behalf of the AEA.

Curiously, Alec missed the flight. He and Mabel were already in Baddeck for the summer. However, their daughter

"To Get a Man Into the Air"

Daisy, all grown up and married now, witnessed the event with her husband, David Fairchild. She sent an exultant telegram immediately, and later on described the day in a long letter to her parents. "In spite of all I have read and heard, and all the photographs I have seen, the actual sight of a man flying past me through the air was thrilling to a degree that I can't express. We all lost our heads. David shouted and I cried, and everybody cheered and clapped and engines hooted ... The first flight raised excitement to the boiling point, and as Mr. Curtiss flew over the red flag that marked the finish and away on towards the trees, I don't think any of us quite knew what we were doing. One lady was so absorbed as not to hear the coming train and was struck by the engine and broke two ribs."

Unlike the first two planes, *June Bug* did not crash, and all the members of the AEA got to experience the joy of flight at its controls over the next few weeks. In only nine months, the organization had managed to create a plane that flew so well that the Wright brothers felt compelled to challenge the invention, saying it infringed on their patents. As with the telephone, there was a protracted legal proceeding to determine who was in the right. Eventually the AEA was awarded their patent, but not until December 1911.

The AEA still had one designer, Douglas McCurdy, who had not seen his work rise into the air. His design was similar to that of the *June Bug*, but with refinements at various levels, including a new type of motor. The group worked on 'Drome

#4 for several months, and soon the end of the group's mandate came up.

The AEA had only expected to exist for one year from October 1, 1907. They had already achieved their goal of getting a man into the air, but they were reluctant to disband when they were so close to completing their fourth aerodrome. Mabel suggested extending the term — and her funding — for another six months, until March 31, 1909, and all who were left agreed.

By this point, tragically, they had lost one of their members. Tom Selfridge, who had had such a close call in the *Cygnet*, had become the very first victim in the United States of an airplane crash, in September 1908. He had left the AEA temporarily, having been ordered by the US Army to go and observe one of the Wright brothers' first public flights. The test of the Wrights' new plane turned deadly as the craft crashed to the ground, injuring Orville and killing Selfridge. The *Washington Post* reported, "The accident was witnessed by a throng of upward of 2,500 persons, who were instantly changed from cheering enthusiasts to saddened and depressed sympathizers."

Selfridge's death was a blow to both Alec and Mabel, who had been particularly fond of the young man. Mabel wrote to Alec shortly after Selfridge's death: "I can't get over Tom's being taken ... I am so sorry for you, dear, in this breaking of your beautiful association ... Bell, Curtiss, Baldwin, Selfridge and McCurdy, it was indeed a 'brilliant coterie' as one paper said."

Alec and his remaining colleagues took some comfort from the fact that Selfridge died doing what he loved. Another friend of his, who was present at the flight, was quoted as saying: "I fancy few men have spent their last hour of consciousness in keener enjoyment. I saw Selfridge this afternoon and watched him as the aeroplane swept through the air above me. His face was set in a smile of pleasure; he was living every minute to its full."

The group got back to work to finish the fourth 'drome, motivated now more than ever to make it fly in honour of Tom Selfridge.

They christened the plane *Silver Dart*, because of its appearance after a gleaming metallic waterproofing compound had been applied to the wings. Following testing in Hammondsport, they shipped the 'drome to Baddeck. Alec wanted to test the plane in Canada, where the AEA had begun its work and where he was already back at work on his tetrahedral kites.

February 23, 1909, was a special day in Baddeck. Schools were let out early and most businesses closed up shop. Just about everyone in town went down to the lake in hopes of witnessing history in the making. They skated up and down the glassy ice, waiting to see the *Silver Dart*. The plane took some time to be readied, so the townspeople amused themselves by having impromptu sleigh races on the ice.

Finally, all was ready. At the helm of the plane was Douglas McCurdy. He had become interested in flying at

Beinn Bhreagh as a youth, thanks to his involvement with Alexander Graham Bell. Now he was about to be part of Canadian and aviation history. He started the engine as volunteers on skates helped push the plane into position for take-off. The *Silver Dart* glided across the ice and gradually lifted off, making a short hop across the bay before easing back into a graceful landing. McCurdy went 9 metres in the air and flew for almost a kilometre and a half at about 65 kilometres per hour. Astonished onlookers were thrilled to witness such an unprecedented feat.

"The first flight of a flying machine in Canada" (and the entire British Empire) was a great success. Alec did not want to run the risk of having any accidents that day, so, despite many entreaties to repeat the flight, he refused. It was too windy. All those present were invited to Beinn Bhreagh for a celebration party to mark the historic occasion. Forty years later, McCurdy remembered vividly "the look of absolute astonishment on the faces of the spectators" as he landed. But the most striking thing about that day, for McCurdy, was the "great pleasure and animation on Dr. Bell's face after the completion of the flight."

The next day Douglas was allowed to fly again, and over the next few weeks he made many flights, some as long as 30 kilometres, around the Baddeck area, despite the frigid February temperatures. The sensation of flying was such a pleasure that he hardly felt the cold. Mabel noted, "On one occasion he was nearly frozen numb by flying at the rate of forty miles [sixty-five kilometres] an hour in a temperature several degrees below zero."

The plane held up remarkably well for something constructed of "steel tube, bamboo, friction tape, wire, and wood," as one description has it. However, it eventually crashed several months later when McCurdy attempted to land in a tricky landscape in Ontario.

The AEA had achieved what it set out to do. In only 18 months, Alexander Graham Bell and his "brilliant coterie" had put four heavier-than-air machines into the air. They had contributed lasting improvements to airplane technology (ailerons and landing gear). They had achieved several "firsts" in aviation. And so, "it was reluctantly moved by Mr. Baldwin and reluctantly seconded by the Secretary that we dissolve, so by the stroke of 12 midnight, (April 1, 1909) the AEA as an association was no more."

Epilogue

Alexander Graham Bell died at Beinn Bhreagh in the early hours of August 2, 1922, at the age of 75. Inventive to the end, he had received the last patent of his life only a few months earlier.

After his work with the AEA ended, he continued to work on various ongoing experiments.

Whether it was an existing device that could be made to work better, or a deficiency he saw in the world that needed something to fix it, Alec applied his powerful brain to numerous problems.

He often spent his weekends on a houseboat moored near the house at Beinn Bhreagh, all alone with his thoughts, smoking his pipe and scribbling as new ideas came to him. He kept up his partnership with Casey Baldwin, who became almost like a son to Alec and Mabel. Several times the two men travelled around the world with their wives, and the Baldwins moved onto the estate at Baddeck when Casey became the permanent manager there.

Alec had been mulling over the idea of a "heavier-than-water" boat for years when he and Casey began working on hydrofoils — which they called "hydrodromes" — in 1908. Their work over the next decade culminated in the world's fastest boat, prosaically named HD-4. This hydrofoil set a

Epilogue

Women workers at Dr. Alexander Graham Bell's laboratory,
Beinn Bhreagh, Baddeck, Nova Scotia, ca. 1914–1918

world speed record on September 9, 1919, skimming over
Baddeck Bay at 113.38 kilometres (70.86 miles) per hour. Its
record was not broken for over ten years.

Late in life, Alec had written, "The inventor is a man
who looks around upon the world, and is not contented with
things as they are. He wants to improve whatever he sees, he
wants to benefit the world; he is haunted by an idea, the spirit
of invention possesses him, seeking materialization."

To the last, Alec lived a life of integrity and inspiration.

His work with the deaf continued throughout his life and beyond, through the foundations he set up with the proceeds from his inventions that continue to this day. His "spirit of invention" lives on whenever a telephone rings or a plane takes wing. His work helped usher in a truly new world.

In his lifelong quest to understand "the world and all that is in it," Alec studied, experimented, and lived with great enthusiasm. When the AEA shut down, Alec noted in the final Bulletin: "The Aerial Experiment Association is now a thing of the past. It has made its mark upon the history of Aviation and *its work will live.*"

The same can be said of Alexander Graham Bell.

Further Reading

Bruce, Robert V. *Alexander Graham Bell and the Conquest of Solitude*. Toronto: Little Brown and Co., 1973.

Costain, Thomas B. *The Chord of Steel*. New York: Doubleday and Co., 1960.

Eber, Dorothy Harley. Genius at Work: Images of Alexander Graham Bell. Toronto: McClelland and Stewart Ltd., 1982.

Grosvenor, Edwin S. and Morgan Wesson. *Alexander Graham Bell*. New York: Harry N. Abrams Inc., 1997.

Macleod, Elizabeth. *Alexander Graham Bell: An Inventive Life*. Toronto: Kids Can Press, 1999.

Matthews, Tom L. *Always Inventing*. Washington: National Geographic Society, 1999.

Petrie, A. Roy. *Alexander Graham Bell*. Richmond Hill: Fitzhenry and Whiteside, 1992.

Waite, Helen E. *Make a Joyful Sound*. Philadelphia: Macrae Smith Company, 1961.

Webb, Michael. *Alexander Graham Bell: Inventor of the Telephone.* Mississauga: Copp Clark Pitman, 1991.

Alexander Graham Bell. Fitzgerald Studio, 1999. CD-ROM.

The Alexander Graham Bell Family Papers at the Library of Congress
http://memory.loc.gov/ammem/bellhtml/bellhome.html

About the Author

Born in Montreal, Jennifer Groundwater moved to the Rockies in 1993 for one summer. She fell in love with the mountains, and now makes her home in Canmore, Alberta, where she enjoys the outdoor lifestyle to the full with her husband, son, dog, and cat.

Jennifer is a freelance writer and photographer, and the author of *Western Canada: An Altitude SuperGuide*. This is her first Amazing Story.

Photo Credits

Acknowledgements

The Alexander Graham Bell Family Papers online at the Library of Congress were an invaluable source of information, and most direct quotes from Alexander Graham Bell and his correspondents included in this book came from this resource. Other direct quotes came from *Alexander Graham Bell and the Conquest of Solitude*, by Robert V. Bruce and *Alexander Graham Bell*, by Edwin S. Grosvenor and Morgan Wesson.

Thanks to Brian Wood, the curator at the Bell Homestead National Historic Site in Brantford, Ontario, for answering my questions about Alec's time in Tutelo Heights.

As always, the staff of Altitude Publishing was very supportive — it has been a pleasure working with the Amazing Stories team. Stephen Hutchings and Kara Turner provided enthusiasm and direction. A special thanks goes to my editor, Deborah Lawson, and my managing editor, Jill Foran. Despite Deborah's and Jill's eagle eyes, errors or inaccuracies may have slipped into the text. These, regrettably, are my own.

Thanks as well to my darling husband, Scott, who encourages and inspires me every day.

Amazing Author Question and Answer

What was your inspiration for writing about Alexander Graham Bell?

I thought he was an interesting Canadian whose story fit in well with the Amazing Stories line.

What surprised you most while you were researching his life?

When I began my research, I knew very little about Alexander Graham Bell, but I thought that the invention of the telephone would be an interesting story. I had no idea how many other things Alec achieved in his life, nor how many dramatic events happened to him. I also was surprised, as many Canadians are, to find he was not a Canadian, but that he was born a Scot and died an American!

What do you most admire about Alexander Graham Bell?

He had incredible perseverance and inventiveness. I also admire the breadth of his interests. He was fascinated to the very end of his life with "the world and all that is in it."

Which of Bell's escapades do you most identify with?

When he is standing at his booth at the World's Fair, watching the crowds go by and hoping for a breakthrough. I have manned enough trade show booths to know that feeling! (Unfortunately, I never experienced as resounding a success at a show as Alec did.)

What difficulties did you run into when conducting your research?

Trying to narrow such a huge life into a manageable story. Alec had such wide interests that almost anything he was involved with could have become an Amazing Story in itself. His work with the deaf, which was a major part of his life's work, is only briefly touched on, though he was very passionate about it.

What part of the writing process did you enjoy most?

Getting to know my main character, learning about him, connecting different accounts of him to create my story. I loved reading his letters to his wife, from when he was courting her and throughout their marriage, since they were often apart from each other. It's an art form that is almost lost nowadays.

Why did you become a writer? Who inspired you?

I always wanted to become a travel writer, and my first book for Altitude was my Western Canada SuperGuide. I am inspired by anyone who can write well and bring a subject to life, whether it be fiction or non-fiction. One writer who changed my life was Tim Cahill, whose columns in *Outside* magazine prompted me to move to the mountains.

What is your next project?

I'm still waiting for inspiration to strike.

Who are your Canadian heroes?

Terry Fox is a great hero of mine. He was an outstanding person.

Which other Amazing Stories would you recommend?

I think all the Amazing Stories have something to offer. I have learned a great deal about our history from these books. I particularly enjoyed *A War Bride's Story* for its humour and for the heroine's pluck.

Amazing Places to Visit

Alexander Graham Bell Homestead National Historic Site

92 Tutela Heights Road, Brantford, ON
519.756.6220

This is the house that Alec's family bought when they first arrived in Canada in 1870. It was here that he had his brain wave about how the telephone might work, and here that he wrote up his patent application. It has been restored as a reflection of the era, as well as a museum about the history of the telephone. There is a café onsite, as well as a small garden on the grounds.

Alexander Graham Bell National Historic Site of Canada

Chebucto Street, Baddeck, NS
902.295.2069

This was where Alec and Mabel built their summer retreat and where he spent a good portion of every year for almost four decades. There is a fascinating museum here dedicated to his research into flight and many other fields that caught his fancy as an inventor.

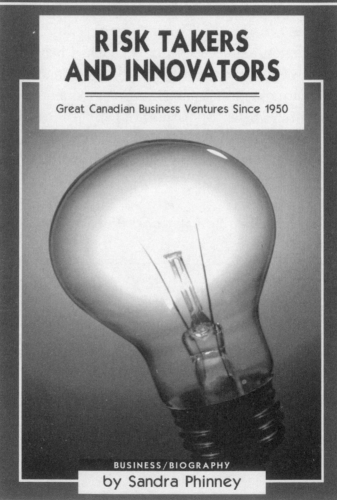

AMAZING STORIES™

RISK TAKERS
AND INNOVATORS

Great Canadian Business Ventures Since 1950

BUSINESS/BIOGRAPHY

by Sandra Phinney

RISK TAKERS AND INNOVATORS
Great Canadian Business Ventures Since 1950

"Surely it can't be that difficult.
After all, everything under the sun has
to be invented by someone. Why not me?"
Roy Mayer, Inventor

Harnessing their creativity, technology skills, and entrepreneurship, the tenacious individuals featured in these stories have realized their dreams and, in many cases, developed their innovation into a viable business venture. From the first glimmer of an idea to the fruition of the invention, these great Canadian discoveries are an inspiration to aspiring inventors and entrepreneurs everywhere.

True stories. Truly Canadian.

ISBN 1-55153-974-8

ALSO AVAILABLE!

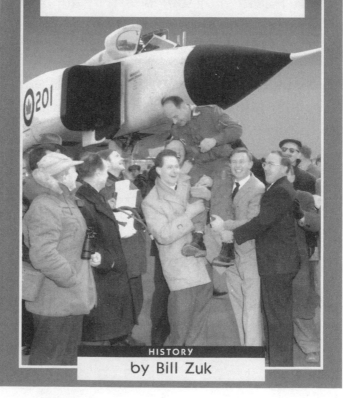

AMAZING STORIES™

THE AVRO ARROW STORY

The Revolutionary Airplane
and its Courageous Test Pilots

HISTORY

by Bill Zuk

THE AVRO ARROW STORY
The Revolutionary Airplane and its Courageous Test Pilots

"These dedicated men and women gave blood, sweat, and tears as their contribution... And now, it really happened, our beloved bird was in the air."
Ray Boone, A.V. Roe Canada employee

In the 1950s, A. V. Roe Canada was at the forefront of aviation development worldwide. After building one of the first jet airliners and completing production of Canada's first jet fighter, the company was poised to launch its most revolutionary design — the Avro Arrow. Despite the efforts of courageous test pilots and some of the world's best designers, engineers, and technicians, the dream was shattered.

True stories. Truly Canadian.

ISBN 1-55153-978-0

OTHER AMAZING STORIES

These titles are available wherever you buy books. If you have trouble finding the book you want, call the Altitude order desk at **1-800-957-6888**, e-mail your request to: **orderdesk@altitudepublishing.com** or visit our Web site at **www.amazingstories.ca**

New AMAZING STORIES titles are published every month.